"Laurence Pope has written a brilliant book on the most significant problem with American diplomacy today. He is an experienced and gifted diplomat who has a deep understanding of his craft. He knows the military well and is highly qualified to address this subject. This is an important work and its message should be heeded by all our political and military leaders. It is a must read for all Americans."—Anthony C. Zinni, former General USMC, USA.

"With style, wit and vivid insight, Laurence Pope describes the current institutional shambles of the State Department and the marginalization of America's professional Foreign Service. The escalating usurpation of national security policy-making by the military, the intelligence services and a burgeoning White House staff means that the United States faces this complex world almost bereft of the essential prime asset of a great power: skilled diplomacy. Pope's restrained, intelligent analysis is a flashing warning light for the nation."—Raymond G. H. Seitz, former Assistant Secretary of State for Europe, former Ambassador to the Court of St. James's, USA.

"A slashing, erudite, highly readable and deeply troubling examination of the problems with an American diplomacy imbued with fads but losing sight of power realities at home and abroad. Many will debate individual points but all should be concerned with the overall picture and heed the call for change."—Ronald E. Neumann, former Ambassador to Algeria, Bahrain and Afghanistan and President, American Academy of Diplomacy, USA.

"Pope's cogent plea for rehabilitating America's neglected and scorned State Department, and especially its Foreign Service professionals, should be required reading for Congress, the White House and thoughtful citizens far beyond the beltway. After two disastrous wars, here's the case for loosening the White House monopoly on foreign policy, reining in the military-intelligence state's excesses and restoring America's battered relations with the world."—Jon Randal, former Senior Foreign Correspondent for the *Washington Post*.

DOI: 10.1057/9781137298553.0001

Other Palgrave Pivot titles

DOI: 10.1057/9781137298553.0001

palgrave▸pivot

The Demilitarization of American Diplomacy: Two Cheers for Striped Pants

Laurence Pope

DOI: 10.1057/9781137298553.0001

First published 2014 by
PALGRAVE MACMILLAN

Palgrave Macmillan in the UK is an imprint of Macmillan Publishers Limited, registered in England, company number 785998, of Houndmills, Basingstoke, Hampshire RG21 6XS.

Palgrave Macmillan in the US is a division of St Martin's Press LLC, 175 Fifth Avenue, New York, NY 10010.

Palgrave Macmillan is the global academic imprint of the above companies and has companies and representatives throughout the world.

Palgrave® and Macmillan® are registered trademarks in the United States, the United Kingdom, Europe and other countries

ISBN: 978-1-137-29856-0 EPUB
ISBN: 978-1-137-29855-3 PDF
ISBN: 978-1-137-29854-6 Hardback

This book is printed on paper suitable for recycling and made from fully managed and sustained forest sources. Logging, pulping and manufacturing processes are expected to conform to the environmental regulations of the country of origin.

A catalogue record for this book is available from the British Library.

A catalog record for this book is available from the Library of Congress.

www.palgrave.com/pivot

DOI: 10.1057/9781137298553

▶ *To the women and men of the Foreign Service
of the United States*

DOI: 10.1057/9781137298553.0001

Contents

DOI: 10.1057/9781137298553.0001

Introduction

Pope, Laurence. *The Demilitarization of American Diplomacy: Two Cheers for Striped Pants.* Basingstoke: Palgrave Macmillan, 2014.
DOI: 10.1057/9781137298553.0002.

▶

As over a decade of war and nation-building in Iraq and Afghanistan draws to a close, American foreign policy is at an inflection point. In Afghanistan, the longest war in the country's history is winding down to an unsatisfactory end. An initial air campaign assisted by special forces on the ground tipped the balance against the regime which housed those responsible for the attacks of September 11, 2001, but this success was followed by years of inconclusive counterinsurgency in support of a corrupt government. The Taliban took refuge across the border in Pakistan, which despite billions of dollars in American subsidies continued to collude with them. In Iraq American military power was used decisively to remove a hated regime but there was no plan to govern the country. The result was to plunge Iraq into a civil war from which it has yet to emerge. Under Iranian pressure, the government we midwived into existence refused to allow us even a residual military presence in the country we occupied for eight years. Only an Ozymandias-like fortress Embassy remains in Baghdad as evidence of our folly.

These foreign adventures came at a terrible cost – upward of $4–6 trillion, an unfathomable sum which pales beside the butcher's bill of combat deaths and injuries.[1] Because they were paid for with borrowed money, the country's economic health was compromised, and balanced budgets gave way to deficit spending. The foreign and domestic opportunities lost during these feckless nation-building adventures are impossible to calculate. Now we face a hangover from these excesses, a period of retrenchment which will contain its own dangers, as the body politic recoils from Middle Eastern wars.

Meanwhile the militarized institutions of the U.S. national security state remain mired in the Bush-era war on terror. A military-intelligence apparatus has displaced the Department of State, and a President who is a former community activist with little prior experience of government has been content to centralize policy control in the White House.

I was a career diplomat for thirty years. When in 2000 the Senate Foreign Relations Committee under the late Senator Jesse Helms made clear it would not take up my confirmation as ambassador to Kuwait – the issue had to do with an Iraqi exile named Ahmed Chalabi who proved to be an unsatisfactory de Gaulle when the time came – I retired and moved to Maine. For a time in 2001 I was the staff director for an international commission set up to investigate the causes of the second Palestinian *intifada* – not much of a mystery if the truth be told. I spent a few months with the American delegation at the UN after the 9/11

DOI: 10.1057/9781137298553.0002

attacks. Mostly I devoted myself to harmless scholarly pursuits. I wrote the first biography of a Frenchman who might be said to be the father of professional diplomacy, and I published an edition of his letters to a great lady in Paris. At one point I declined an invitation to join the staff of Embassy Baghdad to manage political-military affairs. At the outset of the first Obama term I agreed to go to Baghdad as the deputy ambassador to General Anthony C. Zinni, for whom I had worked when he was running the U.S. Central Command, but the Obama Administration changed its mind about Zinni's appointment without telling him – in retrospect a harbinger of things to come. I continued to ponder the War of the Spanish Succession and haunt dusty archives.

The Defense Department was flush with cash, and I also found myself in demand for military consulting assignments. I was a regular presence at various war games and seminars, as the U.S. military tried to come to grips with wars they had been handed by the civilian leadership. There I found an attentive audience for the proposition that warfare is not engineering but a branch of politics. I stopped going after the money dried up and I concluded that this lesson had been over learned, not necessarily in that order. I was also engaged in what the military calls "concept development" – theoretical work involving this new kind of political warfare. For five or six years I was the resident skeptic at a Defense Advanced Research Projects Agency (DARPA) project which had the objective of displaying all the information a military commander would need about the world in a relational data base. (The problem was the nature of those relations, not to mention the data. It turns out that the most important things can't be counted.)

Some of this was easy enough for a devout civilian to dismiss. As one of a group of experts convened to comment on a draft of what is called the National Military Strategy, I asked the Admiral presiding over the PowerPoint briefing whether I could see the prose the slides derived from. "We haven't written that yet", he said thoughtfully, "maybe next time we should do that first." On the whole I came away from a decade of involvement in such exercises with a sense of the American military as a deeply serious institution. Its senior leaders cared about ideas and the profession of arms, conscious of their heavy responsibility for the lives entrusted to their care. It was a stark contrast with the State Department where I had worked for most of my life. Its attitude towards planning and theory can be summed up by Harold MacMillan's probably apocryphal response to someone who asked him what had shaped his government's strategy: "events, dear boy, events." At the State Department, history is one damn thing after another.

The American military is different. It lives to plan, and ideas are important to it. The connection between ideas and the brutal business of warfare was brought home to me early on in my career as a consultant. It was in the salad days before the invasion of Iraq, when everything seemed possible to the arrogant leadership of Donald Rumsfeld's Pentagon. In those days the fashion was for something called "netcentric operations", where "net" is short for network – part of an expansive ideology modestly known as the Revolution in Military Affairs (RMA). The premise of the RMA was that information technology could dispel Clausewitz's fog of war, and a war game known as Millenium Challenge 2002 was organized to test the proposition. It involved the invasion and occupation of a large country with an Islamic regime and an extensive coastline on the Persian Gulf – no prizes for guessing which one. An elaborate (and expensive) event involving the movement of real ships and planes as well as icons on computer screens was organized, and an American force augmented by the usual English-speaking "coalition partners" was assigned the mission of defeating the enemy using a "concept" called Rapid and Decisive Operations – better that, as one observer noted, than slow and indecisive ones. The enemy was routed, but not before the retired general officer in charge of the enemy force (Red Team in war-game jargon) walked out in disgust after the rules were changed to resurrect an American aircraft carrier he had sunk using swarms of small boats. (The U.S. Navy is as convinced that its carriers are unsinkable as Cunard was before its passenger liner hit that iceberg.)

The leader of the Red Team was Paul van Riper, a thoughtful retired Marine General who had commanded the Marine Corps's training base at Quantico. (The U.S. military is a vast and remarkably successful educational enterprise.) Malcolm Gladwell's version of what happened is in his 2007 book *Blink*, but General van Riper's disgust over the premise of Millennium Challenge was the fruit of a lifetime spent studying military operations and the theory of war, not a flash of intuition. I remember standing with him on the steps of a conference center at the Army War College where the exercise was being held. "It's a good thing nobody will ever act on this nonsense", I said. "You are wrong", he said, "they will." Not long afterwards in Iraq, they did, and a few years later, I watched a very senior Army general with a sense of humor take refuge under a conference table when the RDO notion was invoked.

DOI: 10.1057/9781137298553.0002

The Pentagon's faith in the power of information technology to eliminate the messiness of armed conflict never reached the level of settled doctrine – the American military is almost as conservative in doctrinal matters as the Roman Catholic church – but by feeding the arrogance of Donald Rumsfeld and his neocon associates, these cavalier notions about the triumph of technology contributed to the catastrophic political failure which followed the invasion of Iraq. When the American military reinvented itself in the harsh crucible of the Iraqi civil war, it wasn't just a matter of the counterinsurgency doctrine associated with General David Petraeus, or the so-called surge, an alliance with elements of the same Sunni insurgency we had been fighting. The real revolution in American military affairs was the recognition of the ancient truth that war is a branch of politics.

This book had been commissioned when our ambassador to Libya, Chris Stevens, was murdered in Benghazi with three other Americans, and I volunteered to come out of retirement to take temporary charge of the Embassy in Tripoli. I found myself in Libya running an operation with over 100 Americans loosely accredited to a fledgling state. From Tripoli I reported to Beth Jones, an old friend who had been brought back from retirement by Hillary Clinton as her Assistant Secretary for Near Eastern affairs, and to the Deputy Secretary, Bill Burns, a career Foreign Service Officer who had served the Bush and Obama administrations with equal distinction and integrity. Their leadership in impossible circumstances was an inspiration, but the experience reinforced the view I had formed on the outside of a marginalized State Department and a militarized foreign policy process.

As the endless 2012 Presidential election campaign drew to a merciful close, with vile partisan agitprop over the tragedy in Benghazi filling the airwaves, an Accountability Review Board was commissioned by the State Department as required by law, and it issued a report calling for higher walls and more barbed wire. I will not say more about these months on a compound protected by fifty Marines. There will be no tales out of school here, no classified disclosures. The State Department censors can stand down. I hope it is not an indiscretion to say that I came back home with a renewed sense of the need to tell this story.

It is a commonplace on both the right and the left to invoke a so-called diplomacy deficit in the conduct of American foreign policy, and to deplore its reflexive resort to military solutions.[2] This book is an attempt to account for this, at least in part, by examining the weakness of our

DOI: 10.1057/9781137298553.0002

diplomatic institutions within a national security bureaucracy transformed by a decade of war. In the jargon of international relations it is
written from a realist point of view – is there any other? Like the blind
men who tried to describe an elephant, writers on foreign policy often
miss the whole for the parts. There is a body of learned work on defense
theory, and a six-foot shelf of books on foreign policy, but they tend to
remain in separate compartments. Very little has been written on the
way the government works as a whole, and on the intersection between
diplomacy and military operations. Academic theorists tend to minimize
the importance of institutions and the process by which policy is made
and implemented. Practitioners, including former ones like me, have a
tendency to focus on process and institutions to the exclusion of theory. I
have tried to include both perspectives. The unity of thought and action is
a useful goal, even if it is unattainable in the contingent realm of politics.

This book is written from an American perspective – the only one I
know – but its conclusions may be of interest to observers of American
politics in other countries as well. We wield unprecedented military
power, and can kill enemies from thousands of miles with the flick of a
joystick, but we are a sovereign state among other equally sovereign states,
and we forget this at our peril. Foreign policy is not only, even mostly,
about what Presidents want to do; strategy is not the business of setting
utopian goals, but the matching of finite resources to the task at hand. As
our disastrous nation-building adventures in Iraq and Afghanistan come
to an unhappy end, we are beginning to understand that our militarized
national security institutions are instruments ill-adapted to the purpose
of leadership in a world of sovereign nations. Before those institutions
can be reformed, there will have to be a fundamental change in the way
we think about our place in the world.

Notes

1   http://www.washingtonpost.com/world/national-security/study-iraq-
    afghan-war-costs-to-top-4-trillion/2013/03/28/b82a5dce-97ed-11e2-814b-
    063623d80a60_story.html?tid=pm_world_pop.
2   See, for example, http://shadow.foreignpolicy.com/posts/2013/08/08/,the_
    obama_administrations_diplomatic_deficit, by Will Imboden. The books of
    Andrew J. Bacevich explore the problematic of militarization, a loaded word.
    See his *Washington Rules: America's Path to Permanent War*, 2010.

DOI: 10.1057/9781137298553.0002

1

A City on a Hill Cannot Be Hid

Abstract: *American exceptionalism as embodied in the "Shining City on a Hill" trope coexists uneasily with diplomacy, which requires a world of sovereign and juridically equal states. Of relatively recent coinage, the terms "diplomat" and "diplomacy" date to only about 1800. As American power declines in a relative sense in the 21st century, diplomacy will be more important than ever. At its heart is the exercise of state power, not the search for international understanding.*

Pope, Laurence. *The Demilitarization of American Diplomacy: Two Cheers for Striped Pants.* Basingstoke: Palgrave Macmillan, 2014.
DOI: 10.1057/9781137298553.0003.

The structure of contemporary American foreign policy institutions is the result of many factors.[1] One of them is certainly the conviction, which is deeply rooted in the American psyche, that the United States is endowed with a special mission which makes it different from other countries – the notion of American exceptionalism. Early in his first term President Obama appeared to call this into question, responding to a journalist's question by saying " 'I believe in American exceptionalism, just as I suspect that the Brits believe in British exceptionalism and the Greeks believe in Greek exceptionalism.' "[2] To state the proposition in this way was to undermine it, and he was pilloried for his heresy. He later sought to make amends, and did so with a rhetorical vengeance. At the Air Force Academy in March 2012, not coincidentally a Presidential election year, he invoked the notion again, adding Madeleine Albright's notion of the "indispensable nation" for good measure: "And one of the reasons is that the United States has been, and will always be, the one indispensable nation in world affairs. It's one of the many examples of why America is exceptional. It's why I firmly believe that if we rise to this moment in history, if we meet our responsibilities, then – just like the 20th century – the 21st century will be another great American Century."[3] In less bombastic tones, in a 2011 address from his White House office about the Libyan intervention, Obama declared that "Some nations may be able to turn a blind eye to atrocities in other countries. The United States of America is different."[4]

The exceptionalist doctrine has deep roots in American history, but the city-on-a-hill trope is relatively recent. It was introduced into the American political vocabulary by John F. Kennedy before his inauguration as President, in a 1961 speech to the Massachusetts legislature. Invoking a homily by Governor Winthrop of the Massachusetts Bay Colony in 1630 to his flock on board the sloop Arabella en route to the new world, Kennedy declared: "But I have been guided by the standard John Winthrop set before his shipmates on the flagship Arabella three hundred and thirty-one years ago, as they, too, faced the task of building a new government on a perilous frontier. 'We must always consider', he said, 'that we shall be as a city upon a hill – the eyes of all people are upon us.' "

As Winthrop's flock would have known, but we have forgotten, the reference is to the Gospel of Saint Matthew: "A City on a Hill cannot be Hid." Quoting from Winthrop's homily was the suggestion of Harvard historian Arthur Schlesinger, who had urged Kennedy to invoke it as a

DOI: 10.1057/9781137298553.0003

rebuke to corrupt Massachusetts politicians.[5] Wisely Kennedy cited it as an injunction to a higher standard of morality in politics generally, rather than as a lesson to the pols of the Bay State, whose wicked ways he knew all too well. It was of course Ronald Reagan who adopted and popularized the reference, and it became a staple, indeed the staple, of his political rhetoric, from his address to a conservative political group in 1974, when he quoted it correctly, to his farewell to the American people in 1989, by which time he and his speechwriters were routinely adding the adjective "shining" to the city. No longer exposed and vulnerable it had become a beacon to mankind, Winthrop's admonition stood squarely on its head.

These days the exposed and vulnerable city of Saint Matthew's gospel has become the proud citadel from which Americans patrol a restive world. Eisenhower's injunction that "every gun that is made, every warship launched, every rocket fired signifies, in the final sense, a theft from those who hunger and are not fed, those who are cold and are not clothed", is ignored.[6] The Cold War is over, and the terrorists who planned the attacks of September 11, 2001 are mostly dead, but the Global War on Terror continues in the powerful institutions built in its name which thrive inside a military-intelligence complex little understood outside the charmed precincts of the Washington beltway. When military power becomes an end in itself, we are closer to 19th-century Prussia than to the good land of John Winthrop.

Exceptionalism and diplomacy coexist uneasily. Before going any further it may be well to consider a definition of the latter term, though no less an authority than Henry Kissinger wrote a long book with that title without doing so. It is a particularly elastic word – but when Humpty Dumpty asserts with regard to the meaning of words that it is a question of who is to be the master, and the commonsensical Alice wonders whether it is really possible to make words mean so many different things, our sympathies must be with Alice.

They have a spurious air of antiquity, but "diplomacy" and "diplomat" are relatively recent coinages. The Renaissance knew nothing of them, much less the ancient world. They arise about the time of the French Revolution, popularized in English by Edmund Burke according to the august OED.[7] Diplomacy derives from "diplomatics", *la diplomatique* in French, which meant (and still means in some rarefied circles) the systematic analysis of charters of nobility, titles, and genealogical documents.[8] In the first act of Shakespeare's Henry V, when the Archbishop of

Canterbury justifies Henry's invasion of France by tracing his disputed claim to the French throne, that is what he is engaged in. It is a scene usually played for laughs today, as the pedantic Archbishop unrolls his foolscap, but contemporary audiences would have understood that unless Henry's aggression could be shown to be a just war, not only his immortal soul but those of his soldiers would be endangered. Indeed Henry says this himself, in eloquent words which incautious advocates for military force would be well advised to ponder.[9]

It is only much later that diplomatics in this sense gives rise to diplomacy and the creatures we know as diplomats. (The words are formed on the pattern of aristocracy/aristocrat, plutocracy/plutocrat, and so forth.) Traditionalists and sticklers for correct usage like Harold Nicolson, a British diplomat and historian better known today as the husband of Virginia Woolf's lover, used to insist on the obsolete "diplomatist", but a search of the website of the Foreign and Commonwealth Office of the United Kingdom, where grave ministers of state now have Twitter accounts, suggests that even there diplomatists are as extinct as the passenger pigeon.

Diplomacy, however, flourishes, though definitions vary. One useful definition is "the conduct of relations between sovereign states through the medium of officials based at home or abroad."[10] It is about the relations between nation-states – where the sovereignty of one leaves off and another one begins, and how to manage the overlap. The word is used loosely for everything to do with international affairs, but it is not really diplomacy when Steven Seagal visits Vladimir Putin to promote the Russian leader's cult of physical fitness, even though the two men may share a world view, or when the former basketball star Dennis "the Worm" Rodman calls on his friend Kim Jong Un, the autocrat of North Korea. These private individuals do not represent states.

In a popular sense diplomacy is synonymous with tact, but Couve de Murville, General de Gaulle's foreign minister, was joking when he said that "to be a diplomat, it is not enough to be a fool; good manners are also essential." Proust's elaborately polite and deeply stupid Marquis de Norpois is a creature of fiction, though an immortal one. As our friends and enemies know, the prevailing American diplomatic style is blunt to the point of arrogance and beyond, as befits the last remaining superpower. Not even the best friends of the late American diplomat Richard Holbrooke, who forged an agreement to end the war in Bosnia in 1995 by tactics which involved bullying and threats, would argue that he was distinguished by fine manners

DOI: 10.1057/9781137298553.0003

and *politesse*. The U.S. government is overly fond of telling other people that they must do things, and of declaring that things are unacceptable which it subsequently finds all too possible to accept. Negotiation was the term used by the Enlightenment. It had the virtue of requiring the involvement of two parties prepared to at least talk, but we are stuck with the murkier term diplomacy which obscures this reality.

Even American diplomacy requires a world of juridically equally sovereign states – the improbable idea that makes it possible for Malta and the United States to exchange ambassadors. Some sovereigns are obviously more equal than others in a power sense, but diplomacy and sovereignty are inseparable. Without sovereign states, there is no diplomacy. A glance at the headlines is enough to show that in the information age the globe is still made up of these entities, and that they are as attached to their sovereignty as the United States is to its own, though this may come as a shock to traveling members of Congress. Talk about ungoverned territory and failed states is exaggerated. The government of Somalia lacks control over its population and territory, but there is a recognized legal entity called Somalia. The former Northwest frontier of British India, where even today the Islamic Republic of Pakistan's writ barely runs, is Pakistani territory when U.S. drones strike targets there. The remote uplands of the Arabian peninsula in Yemen where a branch of al-Qaeda has taken root are part of that legally sovereign state, though they are not under its control – which is why the Republic of Yemen permits U.S. drone strikes. Terrorists are not virtual even though they may be networked. They have to live somewhere.

In the sense of juridically equal nations, large and small, the modern notion of sovereignty developed in Europe at the time of the Westphalia treaties of 1644–1648 ending the Thirty Years' War, and with it came the resident embassy. It was Cardinal Richelieu of France, that ingenious statesman, who borrowed from the Italian Renaissance what he called a system of "permanent negotiation." Instead of sending ambassadors out for a particular negotiation or ceremonial occasion, he sent envoys to remain in foreign capitals, considering that this was the power equivalent of maintaining a substantial body of troops, and a lot cheaper. During the long reign of Louis XIV, Richelieu's innovation was imitated by other European states, and in our era it remains astonishingly successful. In rare periods of peace in continental Europe, the Sun King maintained some 19 permanent embassies. Today France has 150 of them around the globe, and the United States has no fewer than 250 embassies and consulates.

DOI: 10.1057/9781137298553.0003

At last count there were 193 member states of the United Nations Organization. If every one of them maintained a resident embassy in the capital of every other, the math suggests that there would be some 36,000 of these offices. Most states can't afford to maintain scores of resident embassies; even so the total must be well up in the five figures: Togo has an embassy in Japan, and so on.

International organizations from the UN to the European Union have their own networks of permanent representation. Catherine Ashton, the EU's first (also perhaps the last?) "High Representative of the Union for Foreign Affairs and Security Policy", appoints her own ambassadors in many capitals, as if Europe were itself a sovereign. So for that matter does the Organization for Security and Cooperation in Europe, a Cold War relic which promotes good government in "57 participating countries" according to its website. The indispensable Swiss organization known as the International Committee of the Red Cross has missions in "more than 80" countries. The Vatican, nominally sovereign, maintains its ancient network of diplomatic missions around the world long after the Lateran Accords with the Italian state. The so-called Sovereign Order of Malta, a medieval survival engaged in international charity work, boasts of having accredited diplomatic missions in "more than 100" countries. In the information age, Richelieu's innovation thrives as never before, and there are more diplomats and resident embassies in today's world than he could have imagined.

The principal theoretician of this French system was Francois de Callières (1645–1717). His book titled *On Negotiating with Sovereigns* has never been out of print in English translation, and it used to be a great favorite with professional diplomats, especially Anglo-Saxon ones, as the French like to say – in some cases perhaps it still is. His political career began as an undercover agent in Poland, where he failed to engineer the election of a French King only because his candidate, an impetuous young nobleman, was killed attacking Dutch troops who were trying to surrender. Callières represented Louis XIV in Holland at the 1697 Congress of Ryswick which ended the Nine Years' War and ushered in an age of peace in Europe which lasted all of four years. (He was the junior of three French plenipotentiaries, and as often happens he did most of the work.) Callières is associated with the idea that diplomacy is a profession. Towards the end of the reign of Louis XIV, while he was at the King's right hand in Versailles, the world's first diplomatic training academy was established in the Louvre Palace, leading the

DOI: 10.1057/9781137298553.0003

English essayist Joseph Addison to ironize on the innovation of training "young Machiavels" in the arts of dissimulation.[11] Much of the advice in his famous book remains sensible today. Historical parallels between the American present and the French past are specious, but Callières served a prince whose aggressive policies provoked coalitions that brought France to its knees, and who confessed on his deathbed that he had loved war too much. The Louis Quartorizième version of American exceptionalism was the divine right of kings, and of one king in particular.

There have been assertions that diplomacy is dead in what has been called "nobody's world",[12] as if American hegemony and diplomacy were synonymous. In fact diplomats and embassies of a kind Callières would recognize thrive in the complexity of the 21st-century world of states. The relative decline of American power and the rise of states like China, Brazil, and India, has opened the way to a rebirth of diplomacy, as states compete in a global landscape whose features are still emerging. The international agenda is complex, involving issues from the momentous to the trivial. Does the United States seek access to a person in a foreign state involved in an act of terrorism? Who is empowered to grant that access, and can that person be persuaded to act? Russia has banned American adoptions to protest a U.S. law with extraterritorial reach banning travel by certain officials. What if anything can be done about this, for the sake of the children and families involved? Terrorists in Yemen are planning attacks on the United States. Should they be killed using drones, and what are the implications of doing so when one of them is an American citizen? What is the United States to say to China about the supply of nuclear technology to Iran? Will China use its influence with North Korea to prevent the test of a ballistic missile potentially capable of striking U.S. territory? Kenya has elected a President who is wanted by the International Criminal Court (ICC). What if anything can be done about this? What for that matter about the ICC itself, which seems to indict mostly Africans, many of whom remain beyond its reach, including the ruler of Sudan? Argentina seeks the return of the Falkland Islands from Britain. What should be the position of the United States with regard to this colonial survival? What should be done about the military intervention of Saudi Arabia in Bahrain in support of a minority regime? Should the United States arm the Syrian rebels? What is to be done about the Doha round of trade talks? The so-called Middle East peace process? Global warming?

DOI: 10.1057/9781137298553.0003

The list of such issues is as varied as there are states with interests. They are the warp and woof of international political life. Some are minor and of passing importance, the epiphenomena of the news cycle; some are potentially existential in nature; some can be resolved, given time and good will; the most intractable can only be managed. This usually involves that most fundamentally human of all processes, a conversation, and an ongoing dialogue between states. Sometimes this is formal and mechanical, a paper exchange while each side goes its own way; at other times it may carry a considerable emotional charge, as is often the case with human interactions. States are abstractions; the people who speak for them are not. They are diplomats, whether or not they are part of a career diplomatic service, and the business in which they are engaged is diplomacy. At its heart is the exercise of state power, not the search for international understanding. Reasons of state and considerations of morality may coincide. Americans like to think that they always do. But diplomats are servants of the state, and its safety is properly their first concern.

Notes

1   The Gospel of Saint Matthew, chapter 5:

> 14 Ye are the light of the world. A city that is set on an hill cannot be hid.
> 15 Neither do men light a candle, and put it under a bushel, but on a candlestick; and it giveth light unto all that are in the house.
> 16 Let your light so shine before men, that they may see your good works, and glorify your Father which is in heaven.

2   http://www.whitehouse.gov/the-press-office/news-conference-president-obama-4042009.

3   http://www.whitehouse.gov/the-press-office/2012/05/23/remarks-president-air-force-academy-commencement.

4   http://www.whitehouse.gov/the-press-office/2011/03/28/remarks-president-address-nation-libya.

5   See the dossier at the John F. Kennedy Library, available as a digital file at http://www.jfklibrary.org/Asset-Viewer/Archives/JFKPOF-034-001.aspx.

6   To hear Eisenhower speaking these words, http://www.youtube.com/watch?v=on3KFBXQI2E.

7   The *Oxford English Dictionary* has chapter and verse.

DOI: 10.1057/9781137298553.0003

8   The seminal text is *De Re Diplomatica*, 1681, by Dom Jean Mabillon, whose
    name survives in a Paris metro stop near the abbey church at Saint-Germain
    where he is buried.

9   Henry V, Act I Scene 2. The King addresses the Archbishop:

> Therefore take heed how you impawn our person,
> How you awake our sleeping sword of war:
> We charge you, in the name of God, take heed;
> For never two such kingdoms did contend
> Without much fall of blood; whose guiltless drops
> Are every one a woe, a sore complaint
> 'Gainst him whose wrong gives edge unto the swords
> That make such waste in brief mortality.

10 Berridge and Lloyd, *Palgrave Macmillan Dictionary of Diplomacy*, 2012.

11 Laurence Pope, *François de Callières, a Political Life*, Republic of Letters
    Publishing, 2010.

12 Roger Cohen, in the *New York Times:* http://www.nytimes.com/2013/01/22/
    opinion/global/roger-cohen-diplomacy-is-dead.html?_r=0.

DOI: 10.1057/9781137298553.0003

2
The Decline of the State Department

Abstract: *The State Department's foreign policy functions have largely migrated to a National Security Staff at the White House, an off-the-books government agency impervious to Congressional oversight and public scrutiny. The State Department's internal organization is a management consultant's nightmare, and it consoles itself for its irrelevance with globalizing fantasies and a trendy obsession with social media. The result is a vicious cycle of irrelevance.*

Pope, Laurence. *The Demilitarization of American Diplomacy: Two Cheers for Striped Pants.* Basingstoke: Palgrave Macmillan, 2014.
DOI: 10.1057/9781137298553.0004.

DOI: 10.1057/9781137298553.0004

Like most states, the United States has both a diplomatic service and a foreign ministry. Unlike other states, it does not take them seriously.

The decline of the State Department used to be a familiar trope in American politics. Today it is merely irrelevant. The high water mark of the institution under George Marshal and Dean Acheson in the immediate postwar period was an anomaly in the long sweep of American history, and it is idle to harken back to a golden age which existed only briefly. In those days the Defense Department was a new creation, postwar military demobilization was in full swing, and it was left largely to the institutional State Department to shape the architecture of the new world from the ruins of the old.[1] During the Eisenhower years, under John Foster Dulles the State Department suffered from purges and accusations of disloyalty, well-founded in one or two cases, mostly not, but it remained the dominant foreign policy institution. By the time the Kennedy Administration assumed office the State Department was being derided by the President and the hard men of the New Frontier as a "bowl of jelly", but Kennedy saw the Foreign Service as an important institution, if one in need of reform, and he took a personal interest in it which would be inconceivable today.[2]

As the Nixon Administration was settling into office in 1971, shortly before his death Dean Acheson wrote in the journal *Foreign Affairs* that "for over a decade it has been received as accepted truth in the highly charged political atmosphere of Washington that the role, power and prestige of the Secretary and Department of State in the conduct of foreign affairs have steadily declined." Referring to Henry Kissinger and his expanded National Security Council staff as "a court favorite – a modern Leicester, Essex or Buckingham – served by over a hundred attendants and constantly advising the monarch on these matters in the antechamber", Acheson acknowledged the President's prerogative to circumvent the State Department if he wanted to, but he declared that he would not have wanted to preside over the institution in such circumstances.[3]

At the same time, mindful of the threat from the White House, the Foreign Service was taking a hard internal look at its own shortcomings. A long (600-page) report titled *Diplomacy for the 70s: A Program of Management Reform for the Department of State*, released in December of 1970 and written entirely by Foreign Service Officers, contained scores of recommendations. Some of them had a lasting impact on the culture of the State Department, including an injunction to greater openness and tolerance for disciplined dissent. Its premise was that if the

DOI: 10.1057/9781137298553.0004

Department and its Foreign Service could repair its alleged managerial deficiencies, it could regain the control over the interagency policy process it had lost to the White House.

When Kissinger eventually took over as Secretary, having systematically undermined the unfortunate William Rogers, the State Department's management problems magically disappeared, and he found the Foreign Service a useful instrument for carrying out his will.[4] He valued the institution, and it repaid him with its loyalty most of the time. As Secretary of State, he protected the Foreign Service from a vindictive Richard Nixon who saw it as a hotbed of liberals and threatened to "ruin" it.[5] Kissinger carried out a quiet purge of Arabists in the powerful Near Eastern Bureau, but his senior staff was almost entirely made up of Foreign Service officers, and under his firm control they ran virtually every foreign policy operation of consequence. It was more than conventional lip service that led Kissinger to dedicate his 1994 book *Diplomacy* "to the men and women of the Foreign Service of the United States, whose professionalism and dedication sustain American diplomacy."

These days, critics of the American Leviathan rarely waste much ink on the State Department, much less on the Foreign Service. In the Executive Office Building and across the street from the White House, Acheson's courtiers have been rebranded in the Obama Administration as the National Security Staff (NSS), and there are many more of them than there were in Kissinger's day. Without anyone much noticing outside official Washington, the NSS has morphed into a separate off-the-books agency of government, with hundreds of officials and a score of "special assistants to the President and senior directors", not to mention a half dozen with even grander titles. (A plain vanilla assistant to the President outranks a special one and there are no junior directors.) There are "senior directors" at the NSS for every region of the world, each with their own staff, replicating the State Department's organization – with the difference that the NSS can assert that it speaks directly for the President. Although in theory they are simply staffers for the national security advisor, in practice their role is far grander. They are in charge of everything from Iraq and Afghanistan to global development. Even on minor operational matters, their writ is likely to run inside the bureaucracy, since it may take an intervention by the Secretary himself with the President to call it into question, and recent Secretaries of State have had little appetite for this. NSS staffers may or may not have much relevant experience or expertise. Positions there used to be stepping stones for

DOI: 10.1057/9781137298553.0004

high office at the State Department, but recent evidence suggests that the traffic is beginning to move in the other direction, as beltway insiders bail out of the State Department for the NSS, where the real power lies. One Assistant Secretary of State recently chose a staff job at the NSS, apparently seeing it as a promotion.[6] The numbers are hard to pin down from public sources, particularly after the integration of the Bush "Homeland Security" domestic staff with the national security adviser's staff created the NSS at the outset of the Obama administration. In Kissinger's day, many were Foreign Service officers on loan who would one day return to the State Department; today almost none of them is.

This supremacy of the White House staff over the State Department is a relatively recent phenomenon. The memoirs of George Shultz are a long account of his battles with the national security advisor and his staff. Today that battle is over, and the restrained Scowcroft model under President George H.W. Bush, by which the staff of the national security advisor limited itself to framing options for the President, leaving policy development and implementation to the cabinet departments, is history. The NSS refers to itself grandly as the "National Security Council" in its press releases and Twitter account, although by statute that body is made up of the President and his key cabinet secretaries, not the staff of his national security advisor. It is operational to a fault, drafting even routine Presidential messages and negotiating with foreign leaders often without as much as a by-your-leave to the State Department. Our friends and enemies watch this with bemusement on one hand, and opportunism on the other. Why should a foreign official waste time at the State Department when the locus of power is elsewhere?

Within living memory, the entire foreign affairs apparatus of the country, the Departments of State, War, and Navy, was contained in the same Executive Office Building elements of the NSS occupy today. There with glacial contempt Secretary of State Cordell Hull received the top hatted envoys of Imperial Japan after Pearl Harbor. Today a short walk but a world away in Foggy Bottom, in a brutal modernist headquarters from the 1950s, with endless color-coded corridors bereft of decoration or any sense of place, the American foreign ministry is left to keep the trains running more or less on time. Their destination decided upon elsewhere.

The State Department's influence is at such low ebb these days that it is hardly worth the trouble for critics to accuse it of appeasement. Contemporary criticism focuses on its incompetence and irrelevance,

DOI: 10.1057/9781137298553.0004

not its disloyalty.[7] A recent book by Dr. Kori N. Schake, a scholar at the Hoover Institution who would have been a fixture in a Romney presidency, criticizes the State Department's performance in Iraq and Afghanistan, contrasting it unfavorably with that of the military as if it were an incompetent colonial service. She even suggests, with every appearance of keeping a straight face, that the Foreign Service should stay out of foreign policy altogether and stick to issuing visas – keeping America safe by keeping the wrong sorts of foreigners out. She is unpersuaded by the notion that diplomacy is a profession requiring experience and training. For her, military officers have skills which are unique and irreplaceable, but almost anybody can be a diplomat. Dealing with unruly children is useful preparation, she suggests. Her book has made few waves, and it has drawn no rebuttals from the Foreign Service as an institution.[8]

Many of the State Department's wounds are from friendly fire, the consequence of a wildly inflated bureaucracy. Dean Acheson and George Marshall would not recognize the contemporary structure of the institution they used to shape the postwar world. Marshall's State Department saved Europe from communism with a total of nine officials of the rank of assistant secretary or higher, no deputy Secretary, and one Under Secretary. By Henry Kissinger's day, a Deputy Secretary and three Under Secretaries had been added, a total he found excessive, complaining that the internal structure of the Department over which he presided was impossibly cumbersome – "wondrous to behold", in his words.[9] But instead of spending scarce political capital on fixing the swollen State Department bureaucracy, Kissinger decided to work around it – the same rational choice all of his successors have made. As a result, the organization chart has continued to metastasize.

The contemporary State Department now has two Deputy Secretaries and six Under Secretaries, twice as many as in Kissinger's time. The regional bureaus, six now rather than four under Acheson and Marshall – a modest increase given decolonization and the proliferation of new states in the postwar world – remain the heart of the Department's operations, connecting it however tenuously to embassies and to the outside world, but they are a mere bump on its impossibly complex and horizontal wiring diagram, a management consultant's nightmare.[10] There are now some thirty-two officials of the rank of Assistant Secretary, compared to seven in Dean Acheson's day. The Department's website lists a total of twenty-two "coordinators, special envoys, and representatives" – all of

DOI: 10.1057/9781137298553.0004

whom are supposed to report directly to the Secretary of State – plus another twelve unfortunates with similar titles who lack such direct access even in theory. The Secretary of State would have to use the auditorium if he were to be so rash as to convene a staff meeting with the officials who report directly to him on paper.

These developments have coincided with a loss of institutional focus on the real world. Increasingly the State Department devotes itself to gauzy "global" concerns located somewhere in the ether. Of the 75 senior officials on the State Department's website below the rank of Under Secretary – an astonishing total in itself – only six, the assistant secretaries for the regional bureaus, are focused on particular places. The rest attend to the welfare of the globe in general.

The purview of these functionaries is everywhere, which is to say nowhere. (As a general rule the grander the title, the more limited the span of responsibility.) There are officials at the State Department in charge of Global Intergovernmental Affairs; a Global Partnership Initiative; Global Women's Issues; Global Food Security; a Global Entrepreneurship program, and so on. Why would the American foreign ministry have an office dedicated to supporting global entrepreneurs? What is the point of State Department attempts to create a "partnership" between public institutions and the private sector in foreign countries? The State Department website declares that the office in question "is working with partners across sectors, industries, and borders to promote economic growth and opportunity; to invest in the well-being of people from all walks of life; and to make democracy serve every citizen more effectively and justly" – a tall order for a small office composed of a few political appointees. Along similar lines, an Office of Global Intergovernmental Affairs headed by a Washington lawyer who served in the Clinton White House, is said to "foster(s) diplomacy by conducting outreach to domestic and foreign sub-national leaders, participating in domestic and international conferences to engage state and local officials, and coordinating peer-to-peer opportunities for sub-national dialogue." A recent initiative listed on its website involved "Promoting Growth through Brazil's Major Sporting Events."

Secretary Kerry's Ambassador at Large for International Religious Freedom, a former chaplain to the New York City Police Department, has traveled to China to meet the Chinese Government's "State Administration for Religious Affairs" – the very organization which has the mission of suppressing religious freedom in that country.[11] (It cannot

DOI: 10.1057/9781137298553.0004

have been a productive discussion.) The Secretary of State's Special Envoy to Monitor and Combat anti-Semitism is not to be confused with his Special Envoy to the Organization of the Islamic Conference, or his Special Representative to Muslim Communities. Once established, these offices and their incumbents are rarely disestablished, though they may shape-shift over time. What Secretary of State would risk doing away with any of them at the cost of being accused of insufficient zeal for women and girls, religious freedom, or anti-discrimination? As a result, they carry on zombie-like, the living dead of the bureaucracy, well after the impetus for their creation has been spent.

This solicitude of the State Department for the welfare of the globe as a whole dates to the years of the Clinton Presidency, when the collapse of the Soviet empire allowed a new expansiveness to American foreign policy, and an expanded multinational agenda replaced the narrow security focus of the Cold War. There is nothing wrong with this in principle. Issues like refugees and climate change transcend national borders, though in the end it is states which have to address them. But in recent years the globaloney has taken on the dimension of self-parody. Thus the job description of the Special Advisor for Global Youth – a recent incumbent was the son of Woody Allen and Mia Farrow – declared that his responsibility was "to coordinate and enhance the Secretary's efforts to empower, engage, and elevate global youth issues." (Tautology is not a problem in an Alice in Wonderland world in which a junior official can be said to coordinate the work of the Secretary of State.) The Ambassador at Large for Global Women's Issues, Catherine Russell, is a former White House and Senate staffer who was responsible at the NSS for the promulgation in 2011 of a so-called National Action Plan on Women, Peace and Security. (She is married to the former National Security Advisor, Tom Donilon.) The Action Plan in question commits the U.S. Government to "institutionalize a gender-responsive approach to its diplomatic, development, and defense-related work in conflict-affected environments." What this could possibly mean in practice is impossible to say, but now at the State Department, Ambassador Russell has a staff of 24 to translate her action plan into ... action?

This dysfunctional structure has taken a generation and more to take shape. A separate human rights bureau was created in the Carter Administration to ensure that moral imperatives were reflected in the conduct of American foreign policy, a sensible innovation though traditionalists fought it at the time. Today the human rights bureau is a

DOI: 10.1057/9781137298553.0004

modest bump on the organizational chart. It largely contents itself with the production of an annual human rights report card for every country in the world, with France and the UK receiving the same attention as Russia or North Korea, ensuring that not a sparrow falls without the State Department's scrutiny. Conditions in the Les Baumettes prison in Marseilles are said to be very bad indeed, which one could have learned by reading a long article in *Le Monde*, based on the work of France's own inspector of prisons, which appeared about the same time some junior staffer in Paris was assigned the task of compiling the 2012 report. In Great Britain where the great writ of *habeas corpus* originated, we are told that "all suspects have the right to legal representation."

The production of these annual human rights reports can be internally contentious, and it consumes endless hours of staff time, but the arguments generated rarely rise to the policy level, and the outside world has long since stopped paying much attention when they are issued. They are often an alibi in lieu of a policy, since their judgment is rarely reflected in the conduct of bilateral relations. Thus for a generation the annual human rights report for Bahrain has cited the particulars of the suppression of the rights of the majority of the country's indigenous population by a feudal minority, including torture and arbitrary arrests, without having the slightest impact on the U.S. security relationship with that country – nor would it occur to the human rights bureau to intervene in the operations of the U.S. Fifth Fleet which is based in Bahrain. Its job has been done when it produces a report. Little comes of this routinized annual process of grading the outside world. Once it was a useful source of information. Now it duplicates the work of independent organizations like Amnesty International and Human Rights Watch, but it would be an incautious Secretary of State indeed who attempted to change things.

The situation with regard to counterterrorism is similar. In response to hijackings and other mainly Palestinian atrocities in the 1980s, an office was created in the State Department to coordinate the activities of the CIA and the FBI. These agencies were initially resistant – in the bureaucracy, a coordinator is someone who wants to run your programs – but it had considerable success in its early years, led by a tough-minded Foreign Service Officer with the ear of the Secretary of State, a former aide to Henry Kissinger named L. Paul (Jerry) Bremer who was later miscast by Donald Rumsfeld as the Lord Protector of Iraq. Later it drove the U.S. response to the bombing by Libya of a civilian aircraft over Lockerbie. Today, the State Department's counterterrorism office no longer reports directly to the Secretary of State, and the position of Assistant Secretary has been vacant for a year without anyone taking much notice. Recent incumbents have tended to come from the CIA and the military rather than the Foreign Service. Like the human rights bureau, the counterterrorism office produces an annual report which duplicates similar surveys produced by CIA and the State Department's own Diplomatic Security Bureau. Its website declares that its mission is "to forge partnerships with non-state actors, multilateral organizations, and foreign governments" – presumably in that order. It sponsors a meeting at the ministerial level called a "Global Counterterrorism Forum", a talking shop which issues toothless statements and sponsors regional working groups without significant participation from military, police, or intelligence officers. Meanwhile terrorism policy and counterterrorism operations are run exclusively from the White House.

One important function of these global offices is often to organize international conferences which provide platforms for the Secretary of State and other officials to make speeches – and not incidentally to provide jobs with grandiloquent titles for out-of-work campaign workers and congressional staffers. No lasting consequences flow from these events. The resolutions enacted at them are immediately forgotten, the working groups disperse never to be heard from again, and the staffs begin their leisurely preparations for the next extravaganza. The serious work of promoting American interests is done elsewhere.

Much of the State Department's institutional energy is spent in internal housekeeping. Its Bureau of Diplomatic Security fancies itself a separate law enforcement agency – "the only law enforcement agency with representation in nearly every country in the world", proclaims its website proudly – and it has grown in recent years to the point that it is certainly a law unto itself. DS reports to a risk-averse administrative bureaucracy ("Management") whose officiousness is exceeded only by its incompetence. The last DS Assistant Secretary, another retired officer brought back into harness, was a sacrificial offering over the Benghazi attacks of 2012, but this security apparatus is certain to expand further as Congress throws more money at the problem, treating embassies as foreign bases while we fail to hold foreign governments accountable under international law for their protection.

As a consequence of this kudzu-like spread, the process of gaining agreement to any action within the State Department, whether it is the issuance of a public statement or a telegram of instructions, often involves

DOI: 10.1057/9781137298553.0004

an endless round of negotiation and compromise. Command and control from the top is next to impossible, since it is never clear what button will produce action. When a paper finally reaches the point of decision, it is likely have been dumbed down by bureaucratic compromises to the point of irrelevance. Recognizing this, Secretaries of State have taken to ignoring the ponderous machinery of their department, working instead with a few trusted agents within the bureaucracy and a personal staff, leaving it largely to its own devices. Who can blame them?

This is more or less how it works: is there an overnight press report that Afghan officials have been guilty of a massacre? The regional desk in the South Asia Bureau will draft something to the effect that the United States is opposed to massacres, even those committed by our own clients, but this may not be strong enough for the Human Rights bureau. The Office of the Special Representative for Afghanistan and Pakistan will want to massage the text as well. (Created by the late Richard Holbrooke, it has largely supplanted the South Asia Bureau but both offices continue to exist.) Should there be a statement delivered by the Department spokesman at the noon briefing, or only one given in answer to a question? The process may go on endlessly until an official of sufficiently senior rank puts a merciful end to it, or one of the Secretary's personal staff intervenes and authorizes a statement to the effect that "the Secretary has spoken strongly to President Karzai." More likely, a statement from the White House in the name of the National Security Council will have made the State Department's churning irrelevant.

At embassies overseas, the avalanche of electrons produced by this bustling officialdom arrives every day on computer screens demanding immediate action, since everything is of critical importance to somebody in Washington. All of these messages, "cables" in State Department parlance, go out over the Secretary's name when he or she is in town, but most can safely be ignored. Some of the material in them may be presented at lower levels of foreign governments to polite officials who know the drill; a few, more important, may be dealt with by ambassadors or their deputies; the majority will go unanswered or be fobbed off with a non-response as background noise. (It is an art not easily acquired to know which is to be which, but good Foreign Service Officers soon learn to tell the difference.)

A peculiarity of the State Department's operations is that much time and energy is spent in keeping lesser mortals from gaining access to what are perceived to be important secrets to be shared only by a happy

DOI: 10.1057/9781137298553.0004

few. Outsiders are often perplexed to learn that the State Department's favorite routing indicator is NODIS, for "no distribution", as this designation makes it more likely that the message will be seen by somebody in a position of authority. Readers of the Wikileaks cables saw only the tip of this iceberg of privileged communications of various rarified kinds, walled off from the likes of Julian Assange in exotic compartments, and these days mostly conducted by email or back channels. When a special prosecutor or congressional committee demands documents, the resulting "paper chase" can tie up the bureaucratic works for weeks and months. Meanwhile the internal communications of the White House staff where real decisions are made are covered by Executive Privilege which is rarely waived. The historical record left by these practices will be incomplete at best, at worst misleading or wrong.

Since the State Department is mostly left to run itself in a closed circle, the result is a vicious downward spiral of irrelevance and inconsequence. Even the most senior officials soon learn that their views on policy matters are not wanted or needed. Their staffs pick up on this, and they keep their heads down too. An inordinate amount of time is spent preparing paper for meetings of the deputies of the foreign affairs agencies which convene routinely, not at the State Department of course, but at the White House. At these meetings the Deputy Secretary of State may be first among equals by rank, but it is the deputy National Security Advisor who has the last word. (The National Security Advisor is too important to attend this floating interagency crap game.)

The Secretary of State is outgunned from the start by this White House-centered policy process. The deck is stacked, and White House officials with proximity to the President have the inside track. No wonder Hillary Clinton spent most of her time on the road, appearing at carefully staged events which were often little more than photo ops, trading miles traveled for influence on foreign policy, and John Kerry appears to be at pains to spend as little time in Washington as possible. We learn from the State Department's web page that by the end of 2013 he had been abroad for a total of 161 days since his swearing in on February 1, including 26 days spent in the air – a sensible allocation of time given the limits on his authority which are painfully apparent when he stays home. Thus in August, during the carefully orchestrated preparation of the public for limited military strikes in Syria, Secretary Kerry, who happened to be in Washington, was sent out to read a prepared statement threatening action, unable to take questions, while Susan Rice, the National Security Advisor, was Tweeting in minatory fashion and attempting to lay the groundwork for a military strike which for better or worse the President eventually declined to launch.[12] When the economist installed as the Prime Minister of the Palestinian Authority under pressure from international donors, Salim al-Fayyad, decided to resign in April of 2013, a resignation Secretary of State Kerry had worked hard but unsuccessfully to prevent, this drew a public statement not from the State Department but from the spokeswoman of the "National Security Council."[13] Such public comments from the White House, made at a time when the Secretary of State was working intensively to restore a Palestinian-Israeli negotiation premised on support for the Palestinian economy, make clear where the real power lies.

The State Department consoles itself for this irrelevance with a trendy refuge in social media. This is not always harmless, as it usually involves a confusion between the public and the personal. Facebook, Twitter, Instagram, and the like are personal expressions by their very nature; diplomacy requires speech by qualified individuals on behalf of the state. Setting aside the difficulty of fitting even the least complex thought into a Tweet of 140 characters, it may be interesting to know that the State Department's former Under Secretary of State for Public Diplomacy and Public Affairs, Tara Sonenshine, "encourages youth everywhere to make change", a 2013 Tweet which is probably not meant as an injunction to work in retail sales. It may even be useful to know that she is in favor of freedom of expression in South Sudan, since we can assume that in this instance she is speaking on behalf of the United States – though as usual the question of what the United States is prepared to do about this is begged. But what is going on when she declares on the occasion of Jazz Appreciation Month that "the world needs jazz now more than ever?" Would anyone be interested in her view of April Fool's Day ("a day of hoaxes in many countries"), or her opinion that "honoring traditions and customs is part of #public diplomacy", if she were not an American government official?[14]

The American ambassador to Russia, Michael McFaul, a former White House staffer and a great believer in "digital diplomacy", discovered that confusing speech on behalf of the state and his personal views is problematic shortly after his arrival in Moscow in 2012. At a time when the President and Secretary Clinton were seeking a "reset" in the bilateral relationship, his Tweets encouraging civil society organizations irritated the government to which he was accredited, and a Twitter war ensued.

DOI: 10.1057/9781137298553.0004

The result was that Russia ordered the closure of USAID and an end to its funding of civil society groups.[15] McFaul was engaged in a Twitter "outreach" to his followers when a member of his staff was caught red-handed in a particularly clumsy recruitment attempt, complete with a wig, suggesting that Russian security officials have a sense of humor.[16]

According to a report from the State Department's acting Inspector General – the position of Inspector General has been vacant since 2008 – the Bureau of International Information Programs spent a total of $630,000 in 2011 and 2012 on advertising its Facebook page in an effort to gain foreign audience share.[17] When Facebook changed its rules to require that "fans" had to indicate an active interest in the site by clicking, the Bureau lost almost of its adherents, who could not have been very interested in the first place. Its Facebook and Twitter sites aimed at the Iranian public duplicated those of the Near Eastern Bureau, leading the inspectors to note with considerable understatement that "it is not efficient for the Department to have competing Persian-language Facebook and Twitter sites." Recently the Bureau in question acquired a new Coordinator, a veteran of the 2008 Obama Presidential campaign, where he was in charge of its brilliantly successful efforts to mobilize "new media."[18]

This confusion between form and substance, between Presidential campaigns and diplomacy, is fundamental. The United States is not running for election in the world. Information about the world is the air we breathe as individuals, not a medium to be managed by governments on social media. Attempts to manage it are pure self-delusion. Iranians with unfettered internet access have an infinite number of sources of information to choose from. No conceivable American interest is served by "engaging" with a few thousand of them, particularly when it is not clear that what is being said to them reflects American government policies.[19] Diplomacy (with Iran, of all countries) requires clarity of message. According to the same inspection report, State Department offices and bureaus have established "more than 150" social media accounts, each one in the name of a component of the State Department, but no one is responsible for ensuring that what is said on these Facebook pages and Twitter accounts is consistent with any version of American policy. To mix metaphors, the philosophy is to let a thousand flowers bloom, and the devil take the hindmost.

This unholy cacophony would drown out official views, if it were not for the fact that few people pay the slightest attention to it. Facebook pages are a useful medium for Embassies to use in conveying information about visa requirements or American policies, and in some hands Tweets can even be an art form of sorts, but in practice most use of social media by the State Department simply involves the repetition of statements by senior officials which are more readily available elsewhere.

The confusion between the private and the public extends to treating ambassadors as if they were celebrities to be marketed. In recent years it has become standard practice for newly confirmed ambassadors to make YouTube videos (with annoying and repetitive musical backgrounds) to introduce themselves to the local population even before their departure from Washington. They can say nothing of substance, since they have not taken up their posts, and to do so would be a breach of the diplomatic rule which prevents them from functioning in an official capacity until they have presented their credentials to the head of state, but that does not stop them from being chatty. In his YouTube introduction, the newly appointed ambassador to Spain, James Costas, a former HBO executive, presents his three dogs as well as his partner to the Spanish people. The Spanish crown and state have been receiving foreign ambassadors for a long time, with the grave courtesy which is uniquely theirs. Once Ambassador Costas has taken up his post and presented his credentials, he will find knowledgeable Spaniards eager to discuss the HBO business model, and American foreign policy too – assuming he can speak authoritatively about that, which they will soon discover for themselves. Until then, and even then, it is bad taste to presume that Spaniards should take an interest in his personal life. The YouTube silliness extends to ambassadors at their posts. Thus our ambassador to South Korea, who should be (and undoubtedly is) concerned over the potential for the implosion of North Korea, has made a video commenting on the Gangnam dance craze, involving an awkward performance by Embassy interns. In Bangkok our ambassador is filmed throwing rice to the Embassy staff in celebration of a Thai holiday while the government threatens to implode.

These YouTube videos leave an impression of false bonhomie which barely conceals proconsular self-regard, but fortunately few people are watching.[20] The video introducing the new ambassador to Belgium, Denise Bauer, who bundled half-a-million dollars for the Obama campaign in 2012, and who replaced another political appointee who left under a cloud after he was accused of soliciting sex from minors and prostitutes, had drawn a grand total of 2424 eyeballs to the Embassy's

DOI: 10.1057/9781137298553.0004

Facebook page a month after her arrival, with sixteen likes and five dislikes – compared to a global audience of 16 million for a video of a kitten dancing.[21]

The institution at the heart of the State Department and its operations at home and abroad is formally known as the Foreign Service of the United States.[22] The country's military services are widely admired – rightly so despite the disasters in Iraq and Afghanistan which were not their doing. The Foreign Service conspicuously lacks the public and Congressional support which the military enjoys. It is a tiny bureaucracy of some 8000 officers whose entry is by competitive examination, and it is not in a position to spend money in Congressional districts. (These days Foreign Service Officers are known as "generalists", a terminology intended to differentiate them from the non-commissioned other ranks of "specialists" while avoiding the taint of elitism.) By way of comparison, there are some 14,000 FBI Special Agents, and 30,000 career members of the U.S. Forest Service. More to the point perhaps, Foreign Service Officers are now outnumbered by a total of 21,575 CIA officers, at least according to the budget documents leaked by Edward Snowden – roughly three times as many as there are FSOs, though this total probably includes support personnel. Even at that, it is a telling indication of our post 9/11 priorities that the officers in what is now called the National Clandestine Service outnumber all Foreign Service personnel, specialists and generalists alike.[23]

This total of 8000 Foreign Service generalists who have entered through the examination process overstates the number of people who might be considered career diplomats, in the sense of people who work with foreign governments. It includes some 1500 officers who are exclusively occupied with consular work – the protection of Americans overseas and the issuance of visas to foreigners, important functions but not diplomatic ones; 1200 so-called management officers, State Department-speak for administrators of various kinds; and 1400 so-called public diplomacy officers, the remnant of what used to be the separate U.S. Information Agency. The contemporary ranks of the Foreign Service are skewed toward the bottom rungs of the career ladder, the product of hiring increases over the past decade which have increased the number of Foreign Service Officers by some 30%, but most of these recent entrants are the equivalents of Lieutenants and Captains and Majors, leaving a few thousand people at most to run embassies overseas and staff the few policy positions in the State Department in the hands of the Foreign Service – a lot fewer than

DOI: 10.1057/9781137298553.0004

the ranks of military musicians former Secretary of Defense Gates was overly fond of citing by way of comparison.[24]

One consequence is that a few capable senior officers are being sent to one demanding post after another to the point of exhaustion and overuse. Thus Anne W. Patterson, having served in El Salvador, Colombia, the UN, and Pakistan, is currently ambassador in Egypt, and soon to be Assistant Secretary for Near Eastern Affairs assuming she survives a confirmation process complicated by the Benghazi affair. Senior officers are increasingly called out of retirement. Ryan Crocker, having headed embassies in Lebanon, Kuwait, Syria, Pakistan, and Iraq, was asked to run the embassy in Kabul before leaving for health reasons. In India, the State Department has twice in recent years summoned an officer out of retirement to run the Embassy in New Delhi during extended gaps between non-career ambassadors, a total of fifteen months, because there was no one on active duty who could be trusted with the job.[25] As acting chief of mission in Libya I reported to an acting Assistant Secretary called back from retirement, the Assistant Secretary for Diplomatic Security was a retired officer, and so on.

Assessments of quality are subjective, but what does it say about a career service when the Secretary of State is repeatedly forced to turn to retired officers for key posts? What would we say about the Army if it were to rely on retired generals to command its divisions, bypassing active duty colonels, or if the Navy were to bring back retired admirals to direct the operations of carrier battle groups?

Since Kissinger's time, there has been a steady decline in the influence of the Foreign Service within the State Department. Political appointees now dominate the contemporary institution from top to bottom. At this writing, of six undersecretaries of State only one is a career Foreign Service officer and probably not for much longer – the Under Secretary for Management. Of the Department of State's thirty-five "senior positions" at the end of 2012, special envoys, special representatives, and the like, only 14% were Foreign Service Officers. A calculation by the American Foreign Service Association (AFSA) suggests that the percentage of Foreign Service Officers in line positions at the State Department fell from 61% in 1975 to 24% in 2012.[26] Even the name of the Foreign Service has gradually been erased from the corridors of the American foreign ministry. The Foreign Service Lounge, where officers on home leave could work while in Washington, is now the Employee Services

DOI: 10.1057/9781137298553.0004

Center. The American Foreign Service Association sponsors four annual awards for dissent. In 2012, there were no candidates for three of them. The one award granted went to an officer who protested overly restrictive security policies. His protest had no impact whatsoever on the Department's operations. AFSA has been conducting an internal debate over whether awards can still be given for policy-related activities at all, given the diminished role of the Foreign Service.

George Shultz, Secretary of State from 1982 to 1989, was perhaps the last incumbent to value the Foreign Service as an institution. His successor, James Baker, a thoroughly political operator, preferred to circumvent what he called "the building" with a coterie of loyal aides.[27] When Saddam Hussein invaded Kuwait in 1990, Baker was happy to see the career ambassador to Iraq, April Glaspie, hung out to dry, and his people quietly encouraged her scapegoating in the press. Recent Secretaries of State have followed the Baker model of relying on a personal staff to manage the operation and their own image. None of them has taken much if any interest in the Foreign Service.

Like the frog in the pot whose temperature increases a degree at a time until it comes to a boil, a leaderless Foreign Service with little public or Congressional support has grown accustomed to this neglect, but there have been a few recent squeaks from the parboiled frog. In an April 2013 op-ed in the *Washington Post* Thomas Pickering, an icon of the career service, Ron Neumann, President of the American Academy of Diplomacy, and Susan Johnson, then the President of the Foreign Service Association, declared that "Presidents are breaking the U.S. Foreign Service."[28] It scarcely made a ripple in the Washington pond. Despite John Kerry's memory of his Foreign Service Officer father, there is no indication in his early appointments that he has any intention of attempting to reverse the decline of the Foreign Service as an institution. He probably could not do so even if he wanted, since this would require a confrontation with the powerful National Security Advisor, Susan Rice, over the wholesale migration of the policy process to the White House staff, and possibly an argument with the President himself – an unequal combat to put it mildly.

If Kerry were to grasp this institutional nettle and attempt to reassert the primacy of his department over the conduct of foreign policy, the contrast with his predecessor, the probable Democratic candidate for President in 2016, would be apparent to all – for Hillary Clinton's approach to the institution she ran for four years was very different.

DOI: 10.1057/9781137298553.0004

Notes

1   From a high of 36.3% in 1944, to a low of 4.1% in 1949: http://comptroller. defense.gov/Docs/fy2007_greenbook.pdf.

2   Kennedy's intense preoccupation with the State Department and the Foreign Service is described by Arthur Schlesinger in his hagiographic *A Thousand Days: John F. Kennedy in the White House*, Houghton Mifflin, 1965. See the chapter "The Reconstruction of Diplomacy", 406–447.

3   "The Eclipse of the State Department", *Foreign Affairs*, July, 1971, http://www. foreignaffairs.com/author/dean-acheson.

4   Henry Kissinger, *White House Years*, Little Brown, 1979, 887: "The Foreign Service is a splendid instrument, highly trained, dedicated, and able. When I was Secretary of State I grew to admire it as an institution, to respect its members, and to develop a close friendship with many of them." Kissinger adds that policy direction has to be supplied by the Secretary's office to "impose coherence on the parochial concerns of the various (State Department) bureaus."

5   http://www.washingtonpost.com/wp-dyn/content/article/2007/01/03/ AR2007010301405_pf.html.

6   He is Philip Gordon, who went from being Assistant Secretary for Europe to the NSS where he oversees Middle East policy. The inevitable Washington "observers" admitted that Gordon "does not have much experience with Israeli and Palestinian issues", but they thought "the White House will instead benefit from his extensive inside-the-beltway skills" (http://www. thedailybeast.com/articles/2013/03/25/why-obama-picked-philip-gordon-for-nsc-post.html).

7   Newt Gingrich is, as always, a special case. During the early days of the occupation of Iraq, he attacked a "rogue State Department" for suggesting that democracy might prove difficult to achieve in that country (http://www. foreignpolicy.com/articles/2003/07/01/rogue_state_department) During his unsuccessful Presidential campaign in 2012, he continued to harp on the theme of the need to transform the Foreign Service into a body capable of "defending freedom" (http://www.thenation.com/blog/165114/why-newt-gingrich-hates-state-department).

8   Kori N. Schake, *State of Disrepair: Fixing the Culture and Practices of the State Department*, Hoover Institution Press, 2012.

9   Henry Kissinger, *Years of Upheaval*, Little Brown, 1982, 435–440.

10   It may be admired at http://www.state.gov/r/pa/ei/rls/dos/99494.htm.

11   http://www.state.gov/r/pa/prs/ps/2013/04/208649.htm.

12   For example, this Tweet from Ambassador Power on September 6, before the President decided not to launch a military strike: "Costs of not taking targeted military action in #Syria are far greater than the risks of the limited

DOI: 10.1057/9781137298553.0004

but necessary measures POTUS outlined." Or this from Susan Rice at the White House on September 2: "Will continue to consult with Congress and international partners to strengthen support for limited military action against the regime."

13   http://www.nytimes.com/2013/04/14/world/middleeast/salam-fayyad-palestinian-prime-minister-resigns.html?pagewanted=all&_r=0.

14   Examples taken more or less at random from the Twitter feed of former Undersecretary of State Tara Sonenshine, #TSonenshine. She had approximately 6,000 followers.

15   http://www.theguardian.com/world/2012/sep/18/usaid-moscow-putin-protest.

16   http://www.rferl.org/content/russia-mcfaul-twitter-spy-case/24985988.html.

17   May 2013. The report is available at http://oig.state.gov/documents/organization/211193.pdf. See http://www.washingtonpost.com/blogs/federal-eye/wp/2013/07/03/ig-report-state-department-spent-630000-to-increase-facebook-likes/.

18   http://articles.washingtonpost.com/2013-09-19/politics/42215028_1_diplomacy-macon-phillips-radio-show.

19   Iran has a population of 75 million. The typical audience for the Near Eastern Bureau's Twitter feed was some 12,000, of whom perhaps half were in Iran. One wonders how many of them were working for the various Iranian intelligence agencies.

20   For the curious there is a playlist at http://www.youtube.com/playlist?list=PL B31FC1B762384FDB.

21   http://thecable.foreignpolicy.com/posts/2013/06/11/belgian_ambassador_denies_accusations_he_had_sex_with_minors.

22   Not "diplomatic corps", the term for the body of heads of mission at a particular capital. (This is a losing battle, I recognize.)

23   As Barton Gellman writes in the *Washington Post*, the Snowden disclosures have shown "the existence of an espionage empire with resources and a reach beyond those of any adversary, sustained even now by spending that rivals or exceeds the levels at the height of the Cold War." The total of all ranks in the Foreign Service is roughly 16,000. See http://www.washingtonpost.com/world/national-security/black-budget-summary-details-us-spy-networks-successes-failures-and-objectives/2013/08/29/7e57bb78-10ab-11e3-8cdd-bcdc09410972_story_1.html, and http://apps.washingtonpost.com/g/page/national/inside-the-2013-us-intelligence-black-budget/420/.

24   His comparison drew unwanted Congressional attention to the extraordinary number of military bands, orchestras, jazz ensembles, and the like. See http://www.washingtonpost.com/blogs/checkpoint-washington/post/house-puts-squeeze-on-militarys-musical-arsenal/2012/05/18/gIQAs1WiYU_blog.html.

25   The able A. Peter Burleigh. Other examples could be cited.

DOI: 10.1057/9781137298553.0004

26 Cited in http://www.washingtonpost.com/opinions/presidents-are-breaking-the-us-foreign-service/2013/04/11/4efb5afe-a235-11e2-82bc-511538ae90a4_story.html.

27 In Baker's memoirs he makes clear his disagreement with Shultz's approach to "the building." See especially Chapter II of *The Politics of Diplomacy, Revolution, War, and Peace, 1989–1992*, with Thomas M. DeFrank, Putnam, 1995, 17–36.

28 http://articles.washingtonpost.com/2013-04-11/opinions/38463952_1_career-service-diplomacy-appointees.

DOI: 10.1057/9781137298553.0004

3
Hillary Clinton's Power Outage

Abstract: *Looking for a way to give substance to her signature idea of Smart Power, as Secretary of State Hillary Clinton commissioned a massive study known as the Quadrennial Diplomacy and Defense Review (QDDR), which she considered to be among her major achievements in office. Mostly the product of a turf battle between the State Department and its development arm, USAID, the QDDR failed to address the State Department's failures in Iraq and Afghanistan, and it embraced the discredited concept of nation-building at a time when the White House and the Defense Department were rejecting it along with the country at large. Written under the aegis of an academic, with little or no involvement by the Foreign Service, it promoted the notion of the withering away of the sovereignty of other states.*

Pope, Laurence. *The Demilitarization of American Diplomacy: Two Cheers for Striped Pants.* Basingstoke: Palgrave Macmillan, 2014.
DOI: 10.1057/9781137298553.0005.

DOI: 10.1057/9781137298553.0005

Despite some soaring flights of rhetoric, Barack Obama's foreign policy has been cautious and pragmatic to a fault. The military confrontation with Iran over nuclear weapons which may still mark his second term has been postponed in favor of tough economic sanctions and an interim deal. Relations with China and Russia remained difficult. American naval power helped to hold the ring in Asia and the South China Sea, and the Russians allowed the Security Council to endorse NATO intervention in Libya in the guise of the protection of human rights, setting a precedent they came to regret. An incautious ultimatum to Israel on settlements in his first term was parried with contemptuous ease by Prime Minister Netanyahu, and the President backed down rather than throw more political chips away on a losing hand, leaving it to a new Secretary of State to re-engage in a negotiation which has so far been all process and no peace. In response to revolts in Tunisia, Egypt, and Libya, the President temporized, giving tacit consent to repression in Bahrain and eventually to military rule in Egypt. Having threatened military retaliation for Syrian chemical weapons use and called for regime change, he settled for a deal with Russia which treated the Assad regime as a negotiating partner rather than risking another Middle East entanglement. He extricated the U.S. from the quagmire in Iraq and set a deadline for the withdrawal of combat troops from Afghanistan.

Through all of this, foreign policy was centralized in the White House to an unprecedented degree, and the military-intelligence complex created by the war on terror dominated the national security establishment. For all her formidable energy, talent, and star power, Hillary Clinton was mostly on the outside looking in. As the Middle East negotiator, the estimable George Mitchell at the State Department was outflanked by the inevitable Dennis Ross at the White House.[1] Even the late Richard Holbrooke, a veteran national security operator with a black belt in bureaucratics, failed to dent the White House inner circle, and was left to twist slowly in the wind, unable to convince the White House to create a political track in Afghanistan despite the support of the Secretary of State. (At this writing a Taliban negotiating team still enjoys the services of a five star hotel in Qatar while waiting for somebody to talk to.[2]) From Iran to Russia, from the Arab awakening to the Syrian civil war, from Iraq to Afghanistan, the institutional role of the State Department was hardly felt at all. The President negotiated the timetable of an Afghan withdrawal with his own generals, and the military-intelligence complex deliberated drone strikes at the White House, without significant State

DOI: 10.1057/9781137298553.0005

Department involvement. When the American ambassador to Pakistan tried to object he was brushed back by the Defense Department and the CIA despite the support of the Secretary of State.[3]

Familiar from her own time in the White House with the prerogatives of Presidential power, as Secretary of State Hillary Clinton resigned herself to being a loyal and effective front woman for the President's policies. Traveling the world with a retinue of loyal aides, she dipped in and out of problems without bringing sustained attention to any of them. Where she did intervene – over Burma policy, for example, or in negotiating the departure from China of the human rights activist Chen Guangchen, whose escape from confinement and refuge in the American Embassy in Beijing threatened to derail a major bilateral conference – her political instincts and negotiating skills served the country well.

Clinton took no interest at all in the Foreign Service, but she did leave an institutional legacy of sorts at the State Department which was almost two years in the making. A beltway artifact known as the Quadrennial Diplomacy and Defense Review, it does not travel well. Even inside the beltway, it would be hard to find anybody who has read its 242 pages of turgid and lifeless bureaucratic prose. But Clinton made expansive claims for the document in question in her last appearance at Foggy Bottom as Secretary of State on January 30, 2013:

> I'm also very proud to have overseen the first QDDR, which identifies ways in which our agencies could become more effective, more innovative for the future. Many of the QDDR recommendations are already in place, such as our increased focus on economic statecraft and energy, the steps we've taken on global security and justice issues, new strategies to address climate change, and everything we've done to integrate women and girls into our policies.

The peculiar acronym was an imitation of the Pentagon's long-established Quadrennial Defense Review, one of the Goldwater-Nichols reforms of 1986, part of a commendable effort by the Congress to force the Defense Department to reconcile operations and procurement with long-term strategy. Required by law every four years it is a sensible exercise in principle, though somewhat hypocritical given the penchant of Congress for treating the defense budget mainly as a source of pork. Whether it works as intended is a matter of debate – inadequately is the general view – but from the Secretary of Defense to the thousands of staff officers who engage with it, the mighty Defense Department takes the QDR exercise very seriously. Most of the time the military services

DOI: 10.1057/9781137298553.0005

are able to justify their favorite procurement programs as part of any conceivable strategy. (The B-1B bomber has been described as the ideal weapon for low intensity conflict.) And while the Pentagon may propose it is Congress that disposes, driving procurement toward spending in particular districts.[4] But the QDR process does sometimes result in shifts of direction or emphasis, if mostly on the margins, and it is very serious business indeed at the Pentagon, involving attempts to adjudicate between the rival claims of airplanes, ships, ground forces, and spending on health care, while preserving in amber the Marine Corps's sacred three divisions and three air wings.[5] The senior uniformed and civilian leadership is involved from beginning to end. Defense contractors and their lobbyists wait breathlessly for the briefing slides to leak, and Congressional staffs advise their bosses of their implications for the bacon they hope to bring home. The next QDR is scheduled for 2014, and work on it is underway at the Pentagon.[6] Given the constraints of so-called sequestration on the defense budget, it will involve hard choices and disputes between the services over their often overlapping roles and missions which will be difficult to paper over.

Hillary Clinton's mini-me version recalled Marx's observation that history repeats itself first as tragedy, then as farce. Internally generated, not required by law like the QDR, it was a report to no one – not to the Congress, and certainly not to the White House, where it drew nothing but yawns. Nothing in the way of programs was at stake. The State Department's operating budget is mostly salaries and expenses, and there was no attempt to address politically protected allocations of foreign aid to places like Pakistan, Egypt, or Israel, not to mention big ticket items like spending on Embassy security.

There was no institutional Foreign Service involvement in the process, although a few Foreign Service Officers participated on the margins as individuals. The QDDR was driven almost entirely by political appointees, notably Anne-Marie Slaughter, a Princeton University professor brought in by Clinton as head of the policy planning office – the office created by George Marshall, headed by George Kennan and Paul Nitze among others, now mostly a speechwriting shop. Five working groups and twelve task forces, not to mention a "cross-cutting task force on gender integration", labored for some twenty-two months.

The document that emerged from these deliberations bears the title "Leading through Civilian Power." According to a summary which is preserved in amber on the State Department's website for at least a while

DOI: 10.1057/9781137298553.0005

longer: "The QDDR provides a blueprint for elevating American civilian power to better advance our national interests and to be a better partner to the U.S. military. Leading through civilian power means directing and coordinating the resources of all America's civilian agencies to prevent and resolve conflicts; help countries lift themselves out of poverty into prosperous, stable, and democratic states; and build global coalitions to address global problems."[7]

As this suggests, the QDDR was not really about foreign policy at all. A curious reader will search it in vain without finding even a passing reference to the issues that were consuming the time of the Secretary of State and her senior advisors. The words "drones" and "cyberwar" do not appear, nor is there any mention of Iran or China. The Arab awakening was still waiting in the wings, but the QDDR contains no reference to such issues as North Korea, nuclear proliferation, the stagnation of Israeli–Palestinian negotiations, or the collapse of the Doha trade round, among the many urgent preoccupations of American diplomacy in this period. As the task forces steamed ahead, a destroyer escort of gender integration cutting neatly across their bows, the outside world never intruded on their deliberations. The Foreign Service is mentioned only in the context of making it easier for Civil Service officers to fill Foreign Service positions overseas, undermining its reason for being.

The only reason the elaborate process required the gestation period of the African elephant was that the central issue involved a bureaucratic battle of the kind that gets the juices flowing inside the beltway as nothing else can, a conflict over turf between two agencies with a chronically troubled relationship: in one corner the State Department itself, and in the other USAID, the country's official development agency, morbidly and congenitally fearful of being reduced to a dependency of State. USAID is mainly a contracting operation these days, overshadowed by the relatively independent and more bureaucratically agile Millennium Challenge Corporation created by the Bush Administration which has a budget approaching $1 billion,[8] not to mention the private foundations established by Bill Gates, the Clintons, George Soros, and others. USAID's budget is consumed by Afghanistan and Pakistan plus Egypt and Israel, where long-term development considerations take a back seat to the urgent requirements of politics. Donors like Qatar and Saudi Arabia are much more consequential, and USAID is not doing much lifting of anybody out of poverty these days, if it even did – but you would not know that from the grandiose claims of the QDDR.

DOI: 10.1057/9781137298553.0005

The fact that the stakes were low in this classic Washington turf war did not affect the zeal of the combatants. They went at it hammer and tong, using the traditional beltway weapons of leaks and lobbies, with occasional impatient interventions by the Secretary of State and her senior staff who had more serious things to think about. It was a seesaw battle only a bureaucrat could love. The State Department was ahead on points in the early rounds, but USAID finished strongly, supported by a lobby of adherents of development – many of whom, not by coincidence, were the same private contractors who benefit from USAID programs.

By the time the dust had settled, Washington had long since stopped paying attention, much less the outside world. In the view of most observers USAID won a narrow decision, preserving most of its autonomy and freedom of action. (The section of the QDDR about who does what with the development budget reads like a communiqué between two hostile powers.[9]) Unveiled in January of 2011 to an unprecedented (and expensive) *omnium gatherum* of bemused American ambassadors from around the world, the QDDR was immediately consigned to oblivion. As the Arabic expression has it, the mountain went into labor and brought forth a mouse. The reviews were not kind. One influential defense and foreign policy analyst, Anthony Cordesman, called it a "dismal bureaucratic failure."[10] Outside the beltway and even on Capitol Hill it was the proverbial tree falling in the forest.

An opening vignette was added by someone innocent of any knowledge of foreign affairs in a doomed effort to humanize the deadly prose and illustrate of the QDDR's principles. We are told that we are "somewhere in the world today" – not particularly helpful as a geographical description – and two officials, one from USAID and the other from the State Department, are on a road trip, driving what we are told is a jeep. (American government officials haven't ridden in jeeps since the days of Point Four and the Marshall Plan.) It isn't clear who is at the wheel, but these two agency symbols are "winding their way", presumably beating back clichés as they go, to a village in a "remote valley". This contextual clue evokes Yemen, where the notion of nation-building was in vogue at the time the document was being produced, since then fortunately abandoned, but they have no security detail and the road has not been swept for improvised explosive devices (IEDs), so they can't be in Iraq or Afghanistan either.

The "State Department official" is a he, presumably a Foreign Service Officer, said to be "as comfortable in boots as wing tips", and to have

DOI: 10.1057/9781137298553.0005

a "deep knowledge" of the area's "different ethnic groups", though there is no indication he speaks the language of this particular remote valley. The USAID official on the other hand, a carefully gendered she, is a development expert with "long experience of raising communities out of poverty." Among their objectives is to "elevate the role of women in the local community", which rules out Margaret Mead's matriarchal Trobriand Islands. (One hopes they brought provisions and bedrolls in that jeep.) They are apparently not bringing any of the officials of the state in question with them, assuming that they are in a state in the first place, but this remote valley is said to have "local councils" which ought to be malleable enough unless the menfolk of the valley take exception to the gender politics of this particular pair of foreigners.

Why in the first place this village should be of concern to the world's remaining superpower is not explained. There is not the slightest indication that any American security interests are involved, beyond a desire to exercise a sort of generalized global benevolence. Has it been hit by a drone strike with collateral damage, and do we seek to make amends? In any case, somewhat implausibly it has attracted the attention of the entire United States government, as the duo from State and USAID are said to have been preceded by a whole alphabet soup of domestic departments with day jobs back home, Agriculture, Justice, "and more" – but apparently not the CIA or the Defense Department. These are good works after all.

To the extent that they have paid it any attention at all, most Washington observers have dismissed the QDDR as a bureaucratic folly of a particular kind. No Foreign Service Officer I have spoken to will admit to having read it, but the document is nevertheless worth deconstructing. Buried in its murky depths are two ideas which speak volumes for a certain approach to foreign policy.

The first one is associated with its principal author, Anne-Marie Slaughter, who returned to her tenured position at Princeton soon after its publication – unhappily it seems, judging from her parting shot at the national security bureaucracy for its ingrained gender bias delivered in the presence of her patron Secretary Clinton.[11] (Dr. Slaughter is better known these days for her contributions to the debate over the work-life balance for women, and she has recently been a strong advocate for U.S. military intervention in Syria.[12]) She came to the attention of Hillary Clinton with a 2009 article in the establishment journal *Foreign Affairs* titled "America's Edge", in which she asserted that "in the networked world of the 21st century" the United States had an inherent advantage.

DOI: 10.1057/9781137298553.0005

It was an idea with an obvious appeal to a newly appointed Secretary of State in search of a concept to flesh out her signature notion of "smart power", a blend of the hard-and-soft variety using Joseph Nye's distinction, and Slaughter's essay read like a job application. (As an example of effective American networking, she cited the Obama 2008 Presidential campaign which had just defeated John McCain as well as Hillary Clinton.[13]) A mere five years later, the essay gives off the musty odor of last year's fashions, with repeated invocations of the now defunct social media site MySpace, at the time a favorite with teen age girls, and quotes from Pastor Rick Warren's best-seller about the purpose-driven life, illustrating the unforgiving information age principle that those who live by the zeitgeist, die by the zeitgeist.

Using the metaphor of billiard balls for nation-states as if they operated in the closed space of Newtonian physics, Slaughter argued that in the 21st century these antiquated entities were already giving way to an "emerging networked world that exists above the state, below the state, and through the state." In this brave new world the state with the most connections would be the most powerful, she suggested. Old-fashioned vertical command and control hierarchies would wither away in favor of "community, collaboration, and self-organization", but this would not affect the power of the U.S. On the contrary, while all the other billiard balls lost momentum, as a result of its "networking edge" the United States would pick up speed and grow more powerful – a comforting vision for a great power some would say is in relative decline. Slaughter forecast a utopian 21st-century landscape in which American diplomats would receive "instant updates on events occurring around the world, networked to counterparts abroad, able to quickly coordinate preventive and problem-solving actions with a vast range of private and civic actors" – a vast range which apparently would not include other governments. She also argued that women are better by nature at this sort of networking than men – a plausible enough proposition perhaps and certainly one well calculated to appeal to Hillary Clinton.[14]

Slaughter's fantasy of world peace through American networking was in a long tradition of utopian and communitarian thought. In the 19th century, the French socialist Charles Fourier looked to a future in which horizontal collaboration would be the norm, and his millenarian ideas inspired a number of American communities. (Anticipating global warming, Fourier predicted that the North Pole would be warm enough to permit farming; he also believed that the

DOI: 10.1057/9781137298553.0005

sea would eventually turn into lemonade.) There is certainly some Hegelian and Marxian influence in the notion of the withering away of the state in the information age, and of the much derided (and much misunderstood) 1989 essay "End of History" by Francis Fukuyama in the same *Foreign Affairs* which forecast the inevitable triumph of liberal democracy and capitalism. There are perhaps some echoes of Thomas Friedman's popular flat world thesis as well.[15]

But a more direct precursor was a 1991 book once fashionable in academic circles with the provocative title in French *La fin de la démocratie*, more prosaically in the English translation *The End of the Nation-State*. It was written as the Soviet empire was coming unglued but before the greatest impact of the information revolution, and its author was Jean-Marie Guéhenno, then a career French diplomat, more recently a senior official of the United Nations secretariat in charge of peacekeeping and a professor at Columbia University. Guéhenno predicted that in the new millennium states would disappear entirely, ushering in a new stage of human affairs, but unlike Slaughter, he thought this brave new world would not be a happy one, certainly not one dominated by the United States. Economic globalization and the information age would reduce and eventually eliminate the relevance of territory, he wrote, giving rise to a "society which is infinitely fragmented, without any memory or solidarity, finding its unity only in a weekly succession of media images. A society without citizens, and this in the end, a non-society." It was a work was in the finest French tradition of extreme cleverness – a *jeu d'esprit* worthy of a graduate of the *École Nationale d'Administration*, the same resolutely statist institution which has produced the current President of the Fifth French Republic, François Hollande, in addition to two of his recent predecessors.

Whether a generation of extraordinary change later our world conforms to Guéhenno's bleak vision, the reader will judge. ("Weekly" is perhaps an overly generous estimate of the attention span of the American body politic.) Some of Guéhenno's apperceptions have a superficial plausibility. We do live in a world transformed by the information revolution, and the potential implications of this are far-reaching even if they are impossible to see clearly from where we stand. The global figure for internet access is almost 40% and rising. We can watch with horror in almost real time the death of innocents in Syria, though this does not mean that we agree about what needs to be done. For the most part this global information grid does operate above and below the control of

DOI: 10.1057/9781137298553.0005

the state, though the Iranians and the Chinese and others would like to do something about that. A significant part of the population of Saudi Arabia, where not so long ago non-Muslims were forbidden even to visit for fear of cultural contamination, now has accounts on *fays* as Facebook is known. (But woe to the women who want to preserve their accounts from patriarchal scrutiny.) The Arab awakening spread in part through social media, though more by satellite television. For better or worse, money and investment are global commodities that move with the speed of a mouse click. An international elite transfers money from place to place to avoid national taxes, undermining national sovereignty to the frustration of governments. Corporations like Apple operate internationally while benefiting from their American brand. Silicon Valley despises government and all its works, until Google is forced as a condition of entry into the Chinese market to alter its search algorithms and drop its warning that certain sites have been blocked. When that happens, the company whose slogan is "don't be evil" cites China's sovereignty as an excuse for violating its own principles. International bankers hire the princeling children of China's communist elite.

It is also true, as is often argued, that there have been effective international campaigns by non-governmental organizations to effect political change – the campaign to abolish land mines is cited as a case in point. Less noted is the fact that the networked U.S. is often the odd state out in these matters. From Kyoto to the Law of the Sea Treaty to the International Criminal Court the U.S. is an outlier, rejecting any compromise of its own sovereignty. The U.S. Senate has distinguished itself by rejecting an international treaty on the rights of the disabled on the most frivolous of sovereignty grounds, and if the U.S. has a networking edge this is a peculiar way to show it. A new doctrine in international law known as the responsibility to protect, R2P in the jargon, has been endorsed at the UN, but it is hard to see its practical application in Syria today. The U.S., along with Russia and China, is among the states which have not signed the treaty abolishing land mines.

In short, while the information revolution has transformed the world both Slaughter's American-run utopia and Guéhenno's homogenized dystopia seem a long way off. A glance at the headlines is enough to show that in the 21st century the leviathan state is still the fundamental fact of international life. There is little evidence that its power is withering away under the assault of the information age – on the contrary. The brave and hopeful crowds in Cairo's Liberation Square who overthrew a

DOI: 10.1057/9781137298553.0005

hated regime acted in the name of Egyptian sovereignty. Although the final chapter in that story remains to be written, the generals are back in control more powerful than ever; as the U.S. found to its discomfiture, when it was in power the Muslim Brotherhood was more assertive and protective of Egyptian sovereignty than its authoritarian predecessor. The demonstrators in Liberation Square in Cairo were Egyptian nationalists, not cyberutopians. They chanted "raise your head, you are an Egyptian", not "information wants to be free."

Paradoxically perhaps, in the age of the internet, threatened with submergence in the global mind, we cling with passion to the things that make us different. Culture is a persistent force and it shows no sign of weakening even in "Old Europe", where Lombards, Scots, Catalans, and others seek to reinvent themselves as sovereigns, and frustration grows with the eurocrats in Brussels. Since Guéhenno predicted the withering away of the state a generation ago, many new ones have been created by the disintegration of the Soviet empire in Central Asia and the former Yugoslavia, reinventing nationalisms which had never really disappeared. Guéhenno's own France, the classic nation-state, agonizes over its identity and sees to reconcile the reality of its diminished status with a heroic self image, a corrosive cynicism often the result. The European Union lurches from one fiscal crisis to another in an uphill effort to harmonize twenty-seven political systems and seventeen national banks, though it manages to carry on. The 300-year-old United Kingdom of England and Scotland is threatened as Scotland prepares for a referendum on independence. Russia and China make regular use of the veto in the UN Security Council, and Saudi Arabia declines to take its seat. The U.S. uses the veto to block the censure of Israel, whose Zionist ideology is classic 19th-century nationalism. Palestinians aspire to a state with a territory, not to a website. In the name of state sovereignty and non-interference, Russia cracks down on the operations of non-governmental and civil society groups. China hardly allows them at all, and now Egypt has banned them too. (The high water mark of these organizations may well have passed, as authoritarian governments recognize the threat they pose.) Extraterritorial networks do exist, including the al-Qaeda franchise which reflects at least in part the rage against globalization, but the state remains the fundamental fact of international life. It defies our common sense experience of the world to pretend otherwise.

The other major theme of the QDDR had to do with the coordinated exercise of American state power, an idea which is fundamentally at odds

DOI: 10.1057/9781137298553.0005

with the notion of networking "above and below the state." (Intellectual consistency is not a hallmark of the document.) Again some background in the folkways of Washington is required to deconstruct its origins, and the reader's continued indulgence will be necessary.

In the parallel universe of the beltway, during the decade and more of our nation-building wars it became the received wisdom that our failures in Iraq and Afghanistan were the result not of the folly of attempting to install democracy by military occupation and force of arms, but of a lack of coordination between American government departments. The remedy was to be "interagency" or "whole of government" operations bringing all the "instruments of national power" to bear on the outside world – a militarized conception borrowed from the Defense Department where it had become an article of faith. Within the Pentagon and the wonkocracy more broadly, the conviction took hold that the State Department and other civilian agencies of the government, reified in beltway-speak as "the interagency", were not pulling their weight. The Defense Department and the military were at war, but the State Department was AWOL. In the months following the occupation of Iraq, Colin Powell's State Department had of course been elbowed contemptuously aside by Secretary of Defense Rumsfeld, but as the catastrophes in Iraq and Afghanistan deepened with no apparent way out, and Rumsfeld gave way to the pragmatic Robert Gates, the Pentagon's attention turned back to the State Department. Where were the civilians? When was the State Department going to get its act together?

One consequence was a profusion of proposals for interagency reform, thick as leaves in Vallambrosa. They all tended to treat the State Department as if it were a colonial ministry *manqué* rather than a foreign ministry, based on the premise that its proper role was to be a handmaiden to the military in nation-building. A 2012 study by the Congressional Research Service counted no fewer than thirty-six of these interagency reform proposals from a wide variety of Washington think tanks and other institutions.[16] A curious reader may peruse them at leisure, though they have already gone to the same place as the poet's snows of yesteryear. Some would have created the Washington equivalent of the Prussian General Staff, an idea which had an understandable appeal to military officers who would like to believe that someone, somewhere, is in charge. In the end, their only consequence was to encourage the further centralization of operations under political-military czars in the White House.[17]

DOI: 10.1057/9781137298553.0005

The institutional response of the State Department to all this was understandably defensive. As Secretary of State Colin Powell had campaigned for diplomatic "readiness" as if the American foreign ministry were a National Guard Division in need of more training. His successor Condoleezza Rice bridled at Donald Rumsfeld's charges that the State Department was absent without leave, but she had to quell an embarrassingly public staff revolt over forced assignments to the pacification campaigns in Iraq and Afghanistan.[18] The politically astute Hillary Clinton managed things far more successfully. The QDDR with its "leading with civilian power" bumper sticker was her response to criticism of the State Department's nation-building failures, though the reason for those failures were not examined in it in any way. Henceforth, it promised, the State Department would be a "better partner" to the military, its personnel prepared to dash off at a moment's notice to conflict zones even if it was not at all clear what they would do when they got there.

Little was done to give this practical effect, but some old wine was put in new bottles. The QDDR created new "Bureau of Conflict and Stabilization", replacing an existing office of a "Coordinator for Reconstruction and Stabilization", but the standing body of crisis-resolvers and nation-builders it was supposed to draw on for its interventions never materialized, and it has been largely a paper institution in search of a mission. (Foreign states are rarely prepared to welcome the involvement of even the best-intentioned American bureaucrats in their internal disputes.) Composed of contractors and personnel on loan from other agencies, with little or no Foreign Service involvement, it was essentially dead on arrival. One concrete accomplishment it cited in its first year of existence was in Liberia, where "a single Department of Justice prosecutor helped a national investigation on election violence reach a dramatic and successful conclusion" – a good thing no doubt, though what CSO had to do with this outcome open to question. (The FBI has nine field offices in Africa.) CSO also deployed a "small team" for a time in support of U.S. military efforts to catch the murderous Joseph Kony of the Lord's Resistance Army in Uganda, but this effort was suspended because of chaos in the neighboring Central African Republic.[19] Attempts by CSO contract personnel in Turkey to provide communications equipment to the Syrian opposition quickly collapsed amid mutual recriminations.[20] For all its talk about conflict resolution, the QDDR made no reference

DOI: 10.1057/9781137298553.0005

to UN peacekeeping operations in places like the Congo, Sudan, and Somalia, which have essentially been subcontracted to poor states while the U.S. foots over a quarter of the bill.

There were a few other marginal institutional changes in the QDDR. One involved an attempt to insert some State Department funding into the appropriation for International Contingency Operations in Iraq and Afghanistan, but this has not proven to be helpful to the State Department's bottom line. (There is a risk that by putting part of its eggs in this basket the State Department will take a budget hit when the contingencies in Iraq and Afghanistan are no longer with us.) Budgetary chaos in Washington makes it hard to evaluate the lasting impact of this, if any.[21]

But the QDDR completely failed to reckon with the reality of Iraq and Afghanistan, where some 2000 Foreign Service Officers have served. Nothing was said of the waste of at least $8 billion in so-called stabilization and reconstruction operations on the State Department's watch, documented by the Special Inspector General for Iraq Reconstruction.[22] There was no reference to the creation of a monstrous Embassy in Baghdad which cost almost a billion dollars to build, sucking resources from the State Department budget and requiring a mercenary guard force of thousands to protect, while Iranian influence in Iraq grew apace. While the President sought to extract the country from two failed wars, and the Defense Department was pledging never to engage in a large nation-building enterprise again if it could help it,[23] the State Department was fighting the last war and promising to do better next time.

During the final months of her tenure, Secretary Clinton tried unsuccessfully to persuade the Congress to pass a law requiring the submission of a QDDR – a remarkable instance of an executive branch department attempting to get the Congress to tell it what to do. (So far the Congress has balked, perhaps smelling a rat.) In her parting comments at the State Department, Clinton said that "last year, we came close to having Congress pass legislation that would mandate future reviews, just as the Defense Department has done for many years. In fact, John Kerry himself introduced that legislation, so I'm confident that he will carry on this work."[24] So far, Secretary Kerry has not complied with his predecessor's injunction, but in the end he probably will.[25]

DOI: 10.1057/9781137298553.0005

Notes

1   This has been such a regular occurrence over the years that in Middle East circles the term for it is to be "rossified."

2   "Taliban representatives have been in Qatari capital for almost a year, but negotiations seem to be going nowhere," al-Jazeerah, February 26, 2013, http://www.aljazeera.com/indepth/features/2013/02/201322121225350352.html.

3   See http://www.nytimes.com/2012/05/29/world/obamas-leadership-in-war-on-al-qaeda.html?pagewanted=all&_r=0.

4   Despite sequestration, more Abrams tanks continue to be produced in Ohio than the Army wants, at a cost of nearly half-a-billion dollars – even though it is difficult to foresee any tanks battles in our future. The same is true for C-130 aircraft built in Georgia, which continue to be produced despite an attempt in 2006 by Secretary of Defense Rumsfeld to shut down the production line. http://www.huffingtonpost.com/2013/04/28/abrams-tank-congress-army_n_3173717.html.

5   This is only legislative requirement of its kind, the product of President Truman's ill-advised attempt to subordinate the Marine Corps to the Navy after World War II. In a famous letter to a Congressman in 1950, Truman wrote that the Marine Corps "is the Navy's police force and as long as I am President that is what it will remain. They have a propaganda machine that is almost equal to Stalin's." He was obliged to recant, and the outraged reaction from Marines and their supporters tended to make his point. http://www.trumanlibrary.org/publicpapers/index.php?pid=864.

6   For an example of the former, see the elaborate CSIS exercise at http://csis.org/files/publication/130319_Murdock_Preparing2014QDR_Web.pdf.

7   http://www.state.gov/s/dmr/qddr/. The Executive Summary alone is nineteen pages.

8   The MCC is managed by "a chief executive officer, who is part of the nine-member Board of Directors. The Secretary of State, the Secretary of the Treasury, the U.S. Trade Representative, and the USAID Administrator serve on the board along with four private sector representatives." USAID, by contrast, is an "independent federal government agency that receives overall foreign policy guidance from the Secretary of State" (http://foreignassistance.gov).

9   From page 113: "To ensure coordination between State and USAID, the Director of Foreign Assistance Resources will analyze and integrate all foreign assistance budget proposals for the Secretary's approval and ensure that the development perspective is heard throughout the budget process, including though USAID participation in relevant meetings and exchanges with the White House Office of Management and Budget. The Secretary will continue to submit an integrated State/USAID Congressional

DOI: 10.1057/9781137298553.0005

Budget Justification that includes integrated country justifications while clearly identifying which agency will implement which resources." Rough translation: no back door deals between State and OMB at USAID's expense.

10 http://csis.org/publication/quadrennial-diplomacy-and-development-review-qddr: "... little more than a collection of buzzwords like 'civilian power,' '21st Century challenges,' etc. Its recommendations are little more than a morass of new organizational initiatives (and growth) within the State Department, conceptual slogans, and self-seeking politically correct rhetoric. To the extent that the Executive Summary does make recommendations for action, they look like a compendium of slogans and maxims from business schools and textbooks on public administration. In practice, they amount to little more than another vacuous government report calling for clearer lines of responsibility and leadership, more coordination, better strategy, better people, and better planning and management – recommendations that are unquestionably valid in broad terms and meaningless in dealing with urgent, real-world needs in the field." (It is unclear whether Mr. Cordesman made it past the Executive Summary.)

11 http://www.politico.com/blogs/laurarozen/0211/Policy_Planning_chief_AnneMarie_Slaughter_signs_off.html: "We are slowly beginning to focus on societies as much as on states.... Unfortunately, the people who focus on those two worlds here in Washington are still too often very different groups. The world of states is still the world of high politics, hard power, realpolitik, and, largely, men. The world of societies is still too often the world of low politics, soft power, human rights, democracy, and development, and, largely, women." Slaughter has recently declared that she is now uncomfortable in the "contemporary political science space", and she has taken a job heading a leading Washington think tank, the New America Foundation. http://articles.washingtonpost.com/2013-04-07/lifestyle/38354033_1_new-ideas-work-and-family-foreign-policy-expert.

12 For example, http://www.theatlantic.com/magazine/archive/2012/07/why-women-still-cant-have-it-all/309020/. For her advocacy of a Syrian intervention, see http://articles.washingtonpost.com/2013-04-26/opinions/38843130_1_hutus-rwanda-genocide-convention.

13 "America's Edge, Power in the Networked Century", *Foreign Affairs*, January/February 2009.

14 Ibid., 21.

15 Thomas Friedman, *The World Is Flat: A Brief History of the Twenty-First Century,* Farrar, Straus and Giroux, 2005.

16 Congressional Research Service, *Building Civilian Interagency Capacity for Missions Abroad: Key Proposals and Issues for Congress,* February 9, 2012.

17 The classic insider's account is Peter van Buren's lively and funny account the follies of the Iraq reconstruction program. A consular officer by trade, van

DOI: 10.1057/9781137298553.0005

Buren was hounded out of the State Department in retribution for his truth-telling, and his security clearance was revoked on the flimsiest of grounds. (*We Meant Well: How I Helped Lose the Battle for the Hearts and Minds of the Iraqi People,* Metropolitan Books, 2011.)

18   Refer to Condoleezza Rice's memoir, *No Higher Honor: A Memoir of My Years in Washington,* Broadway Paperbacks, 2011.

19   http://www.guardian.co.uk/world/2013/apr/09/joseph-kony-lra-hunt-suspended.

20   See http://articles.washingtonpost.com/2012-08-20/world/35492959_1_syrian-activists-syrian-opposition-syrian-rebels, and http://thecable. foreignpolicy.com/posts/2013/03/13/how_the_new_60_million_of_syria_aid_is_being_spent, which reports that of some $60 million in aid to the Syrian opposition announced on February 28, CSO would spend $6 million in "training programs."

21   The State Department's 2014 budget request was 6% less than in previous years as a result of a reduction in the OCO account, an indication that these chickens are already coming home to roost. This cut is certain to be further reduced by the impact of sequestration, and increased security costs after Benghazi will further erode the State Department's core operations. See http://thecable.foreignpolicy.com/posts/2013/04/10/budget_day_state_department_reducing_role_in_iraq_and_afghanistan_in_2014.

22   See http://www.sigir.mil/learningfromiraq/.

23   See, for example, the study commissioned by General Dempsey and published in June of 2012, titled "Enduring Lessons from the Past Decade of Operations", available at http://blogs.defensenews.com/saxotech-access/pdfs/decade-of-war-lessons-learned.pdf. It contains the admission that the military's early failures in Iraq were the result of its "failure to understand the operational environment." This self-criticism is the product of a self-confident institution.

24   On January 30, 2013. http://www.state.gov/secretary/rm/2013/01/203507.htm

25   When he does, Kerry may have to focus on the Foreign Service, if only to distinguish himself from his predecessor. This would be popular in some circles in the "building", but far from all, and it would scramble some bureaucratic eggs. Kerry's director of policy planning, David McKean, was involved in the first QDDR from his post as the staff director of Kerry's Senate Foreign Relations Committee. According to Professor Slaughter, "I take David's appointment as an important signal that Secretary Kerry intends to continue and build on Secretary Clinton's decision to have a Quadrennial Diplomacy and Development Review." http://thecable.foreignpolicy.com/posts/2013/02/20/david_mckean_to_be_state_department_director_of_policy_planning.

DOI: 10.1057/9781137298553.0005

4
Drones, Cyberwar, Special Forces, and Other Extraterritorials

Abstract: *While a demoralized State Department promises to do a better job of fighting the last war, a self-confident military-intelligence complex which has filled the void left by its retreat looks to the future. Its extraterritorial ambitions include offensive operations in cyberspace, the use of special forces, and drones. The Special Operations Command has a presence in "more than 100" countries, and it is expanding its operations in Africa, the domain of the newest combatant command, AFRICOM. The weakness of the State Department and its Foreign Service invites the intrusion of the military-intelligence complex into the political realm.*

Pope, Laurence. *The Demilitarization of American Diplomacy: Two Cheers for Striped Pants.* Basingstoke: Palgrave Macmillan, 2014.
DOI: 10.1057/9781137298553.0006.

While a demoralized State Department promises to do a better job of fighting the last war, a self-confident military-intelligence complex looks to the future. The State Department may pretend to believe that the sovereignty of other states is destined to wither away; at the Defense Department, where serious foreign policy is conducted, there are plans to accelerate the process through the untrammeled exercise of American military power. The technology-dependent Navy and Air Force have joined forces to embrace the new concept of the Air Sea Battle,[1] a formula for high-tech war with Iran and China, with the goal of overcoming what are known as "anti-access/area-denial challenges." A2/AD is the deliberately obscure acronym – in plain English, the perverse resistance of states like China and Iran to invasions of their territory. The Army and the Marine Corps are not quite as enthusiastic about this, having borne the brunt of the Iraq and Afghanistan conflicts with boots on foreign soil, but all the military services are busy preparing for what is termed, a little like a bad cold, an era of "persistent conflict."[2] Some retrenchment is inevitable after the excesses of the past decade, but despite the budget cuts known as sequestration the iron triangle of the military services, the Congress, and defense contractors will be resistant to fundamental change.[3] The national security apparatus built during the Cold War and reinforced to meet the terrorist threat has an inherent need to find new reasons for being, and new threats to counter.

Cyberspace is a growth area – not the cyberutopia of the State Department, but the cyberspace which is a new military domain of conflict. A former CIA and NSA Director, Michael Hayden, has conceded that the United States "could be fairly charged with the militarization of the World Wide Web." Russia and China are both attacking U.S. networks as well, and unless norms can be agreed, future generations may look back on the present as a golden age before the internet became a global battlefield. There have already been a number of undeclared wars in cyberspace, including the Russian attack in 2007 on Estonia – a NATO member entitled under Article 5 of the Atlantic Treaty to invoke its right to collective self-defense which made that an attack on the United States as well. Chinese attacks on networks in the U.S. have become more than an irritant in bilateral relations. The Stuxnet virus deployed by Israel and the U.S. against Iran as part of a highly classified operation called Olympic Games has been the subject of extraordinary (and damaging) leaks to David Sanger of the *New York Times*,[4] resulting in the withdrawal of a security clearance from one retired four star

DOI: 10.1057/9781137298553.0006

Marine who was once a leading candidate to be Chairman of the Joint Staff.[5] Thanks to the disclosure of the classified intelligence budget proposal for fiscal year 2012 by Edward Snowden, we know that the U.S. carried out an astonishing total of 231 offensive operations in cyberspace in 2011, with some $652 million spent on the implantation of covert implants in targeted computer networks.[6] Though many of these operations are presumably minor, this is still undeclared clandestine warfare on a very large scale, and it has caused unprecedented trouble in our relations with key friends and allies, from Germany to Brazil.

The rubicon of offensive cyberattacks having been crossed, teams are being formed at the regional commands to incorporate offensive operations in cyberspace into their contingency war plans. General Keith Alexander of the U.S. Cyber Command speaks of "normalizing" cyber operations, blurring the distinction between offensive and defensive use, admittedly not an easy one to draw.[7] His new Cyber Command is technically subordinate to the Strategic Command in Omaha which maintains the nuclear triad, but he is a full general officer and largely independent in practice as the Director of the National Security Agency at Fort Meade. This gives him (and his successors) unprecedented military and civilian reach, and he has requested an exponential increase in staff. The Director of National Intelligence, Larry Clapper, made the threat in cyberspace the centerpiece of recent Senate testimony.[8]

Cyberspace is a global commons like the high seas and the outer space, with the difference that as General Alexander has noted "every server, fiber-optic line, cell tower, thumb drive, router, and laptop is owned by someone and resides in some physical locale."[9] The law of nations dates to the 17th century, the *ius gentium* of Hugo Grotius; this emerging virtual world has emerged in the 21st century without an agreed framework of law to govern it, and a strong bias toward anarchy. The cyberoptimists of Silicon Valley are counterbalanced by cyberpessimists inside the military-intelligence complex who see a threat around every corner, and they dwell in parallel universes.

What is needed is an international attempt to negotiate new international norms with teeth, and this should be a central task for 21st-century American diplomacy As new military and intelligence capabilities have been created in the information age, our dependence on them has grown and with it our vulnerability, creating a threat not only to military operations but to everything we do. An existential attack on the U.S. in the 21st century is more likely to come in cyberspace than from terrorism,

DOI: 10.1057/9781137298553.0006

the proliferation of nuclear weapons, or the rise of a conventional peer competitor, and the foreign policy questions this raises are fundamental. If cyberspace is the nuclear question of the 21st century, where are its civilian theorists, its Nitzes and Kissingers? Who will be its Grotius?

In its current decline, the State Department is wholly unsuited to this task. In Cold War days, negotiations with the Soviet Union over nuclear weapons were centered in the State Department. Today its Political-Military bureau, once a serious operation, is relegated to the processing of export licenses for weapons. A small State Department office on cyber issues created in 2011 is focused exclusively on criminal matters and freedom of expression. (The Coordinator is a former assistant U.S. attorney, said to work extensively with the "interagency", but there is no mention of the Cyber Command which outguns him many times over in bureaucratic clout.[10]) A review of cyber policy commissioned by the White House contains no reference to this office or indeed to the State Department, and as usual it centralizes everything in the White House.[11] The State Department appears to be playing no role in dealing with one of the central diplomatic problems of the 21st century.

The debate over drones is another instance of the State Department's irrelevance. Command and control of armed drones was developed during the war on terror as a hybrid of military and intelligence operations, sometimes governed by an intelligence finding notified to Congressional oversight committees, at other times managed by the relevant combatant commander as part of his war-fighting responsibilities. This blurring of what should be distinct authorities for covert action and military operations is a particularly troublesome aspect of the drone program. Recently it has been announced that responsibility is being moved to the military, and the President has promised greater transparency, but it is far from clear what the practical aspect of these changes will be.[12] We learn from published accounts that President Obama personally reviews all names on the "kill list" for drone attacks to ensure that they meet specific criteria, an appropriate assumption of political responsibility by the commander in chief, but the exponential increase in drone attacks in recent years clearly comes at a price, and resistance to them is growing at home and abroad.[13]

Proposals for a special court to rule on drone attacks betray intellectual confusion. Their use is an act of war, not a wiretap to be authorized as part of a criminal prosecution. The Obama Administration's Justice Department has justified the drone attack against an American citizen in

Yemen on the grounds that the U.S. is in a state of war with the terrorist organization known as al-Qaeda. Will the existence of terrorists who claim al-Qaeda parentage in Africa and elsewhere justify a permanent state of war, until every individual in them is eliminated? As sophisticated drones used as weapons become available to other states, as they will, what international rules will govern their use, and will we agree ourselves to be bound by them? What precedents have we created which will come back to haunt us?

Of contemporary American military institutions, the most influential is probably the Special Operations Command (SOCOM), based in Tampa. SOCOM was created by the Goldwater-Nichols reforms of 1986, part of an attempt by the Congress to break down service parochialism and give new prominence to special operations. It was initially resented by the services, particularly the Marine Corps, which saw it as a threat, as well as by the big Army of tanks and heavy divisions. Today these battles are a memory, and SOCOM conducts operations in every part of the world. Its authorities are unique, and its reach is global. Over the last decade of war, the SOCOM budget has quadrupled, and there has been a doubling of its end strength to the present 66,000. (SOCOM is the parent organization, not to be confused with the subordinate Joint Special Operations Command, or JSOC, where so-called Tier One capabilities reside – Seal Teams, Delta, and the like.) SOCOM is unique among the combatant commands in having its own procurement budget, funded in the amount of at least $1.8 billion in fiscal year 2012.

SOCOM's operations around the world are sometimes portrayed as foreign assistance, but their purpose is the training and area familiarization of special forces for intervention of one kind or another. The word for this is "engagement", a bloodless and neutral term which is a beltway favorite.[14] Who could be opposed to engaging with the outside world? In the last fiscal year, SOCOM was "engaged" in "more than 100 countries worldwide."[15] Some of its programs are delivered by what are known as "civil-military support elements", seventeen of which are said to be providing assistance around the world to "refugees, displaced persons, populations at risk" as well as "humanitarian or disaster assistance." These intrusions into what might be thought to be civilian spheres of activity are not motivated by humanitarian concerns; whether they do good or not is incidental. Their purpose is to acculturate and familiarize special forces personnel with environments in which they may be called on to operate. According to Congressional testimony by the SOCOM

DOI: 10.1057/9781137298553.0006

commander, a total of 26 propaganda teams around the world, known as MISTs, for Military Information Support Teams, are in embassies to "support the Department of State by augmenting and broadening their (*sic*) public diplomacy efforts" – a mission which among other things involves planting articles in local newspapers, as part of what are known as "information operations."[16]

Building on the success of the killing of Osama Bin Laden, the SOCOM commander Admiral William McRaven is said to be seeking to create a formalized global network of his own circumventing the regional commanders. According to David Ignatius in the *Washington Post*, based on what was obviously extensive backgrounding by SOCOM and McRaven himself: "To fight the small wars, McRaven offers his agile, stealthy and highly lethal network of commandos. Often their missions will involve training and partnering with other nations, rather than shooting. Sometimes, their activities may look like USAID development assistance or CIA political action." As Ignatius points out, "USAID is more of a development contractor than an operational agency; the State Department's Bureau of Conflict and Stabilization Operations is too small to lead even its own department's efforts, let alone the government's... And the CIA wants to do less covert action, not more. Enter the Special Operations Forces."[17]

In recent years SOCOM has expanded its operations in Africa, the domain of latest four star Combatant Command, AFRICOM, created in 2007 and based in Germany. Six years after its creation, AFRICOM has already acquired responsibility for two small wars on the continent and counting, one in the Horn of Africa, and another in Mali. Its establishment was resisted by the State Department and its Bureau of African Affairs, concerned over the militarization of the U.S. approach to the continent, and Africans have been suspicious of AFRICOM's desire to "partner" with them. With the possible exception of South Africa, no African state has the infrastructure required to host the command, and its headquarters are likely to remain in Germany, but it established substantial beachheads or "forwards headquarters" on the continent. From Camp Lemonnier in Djibouti, a formerly austere French Foreign Legion base now equipped with the infrastructure to support some 3,000 American troops, AFRICOM's Combined Joint Task Force-Horn of Africa (CJTF-HOA) has intervened in Somalia, Ethiopia, and Kenya, operating drone strikes from Djibouti against terrorist targets, and carrying out other direct action missions from offshore.[18] Its initial intervention in Somalia in support of the invasion of that country by Ethiopian "peacekeepers" produced distinctly mixed results. The al-Qaeda-linked al-Shabab has been weakened, and a government of sorts installed in Mogadishu, but the war AFRICOM is fighting in East Africa through proxies shows no sign of ending any time soon, as the September 21, 2013, attack by al-Shabab on the Westgate Mall in Nairobi demonstrates.

CJTF-HOA is the model for AFRICOM's other major initiative, the Trans Sahara Counter Terrorism Partnership in the Sahel, the zone across Northern Africa where for hundreds of years Islam has been spread by missionaries, sometimes finding acceptance, sometimes resistance. A wiki-leaked cable described a meeting in Bamako in October of 2009 between the Deputy AFRICOM commander and the American ambassador, who objected to a program code-named Oasis Enabler involving the conduct by U.S. Special Forces of counterterrorism operations in Mali. In April of 2012, these operations went badly wrong when a Special Forces-trained Malian Army unit staged a coup against the elected government, and the U.S. was forced to suspend all military assistance. A few weeks later, an accident resulted in the death of three military U.S. personnel, who drove off a bridge in Bamako at 5 AM. (Three Moroccan women traveling with them were also killed.) One of the Americans who died was an expert in the intercepting of communications, making it difficult to explain what they were still doing there despite the suspension of military assistance. Subsequently the unit of the Malian Army trained by AFRICOM collapsed in the face of a rebellion by Touareg rebels, who took over the equipment provided including vehicles with sophisticated satellite communications.[19] The Benghazi attacks of September 11/12, 2012, and the subsequent attack in February of 2013 by an al-Qaeda-branded group on an Algerian natural gas facility in the Sahara, have brought AFRICOM additional resources as well as increased policy focus, and a drone base has been set up in neighboring Niger.[20] In response to the Benghazi attack, AFRICOM has been given its own quick reaction force, and in General David Rodriguez it has an aggressive new commander.

AFRICOM is only the youngest (and one of the smallest) of the Defense Department's combatant commands spanning the globe, dividing it into what are called "areas of responsibility" as if the world were one vast battlefield in accordance with what is known inside the Pentagon as the "unified command plan." Their four star commanders are the secular Cardinals of the American national security establishment. Donald Rumsfeld banned the reference to them as CINCs, or commanders in chief, but that is what they remain in all but name. CENTCOM, the Middle East command whose peculiar name echoes the old Baghdad Pact, is perhaps the most politically sensitive, and it has been responsible for the wars in Iraq and Afghanistan. It is based at a newly built $80 million headquarters in Tampa, and its last three commanders, Admiral William Fallon, Army General David Petraeus, and Marine General James Mattis, have all been removed before the expiration of the standard term of three years, reflecting its political sensitivity. Fallon's downfall resulted from an injudicious interview in which he referred to his efforts to contain the plans of the Bush Administration to attack Iran. Petraeus left to take over the war in Afghanistan after the firing of his titular subordinate, General Stanley McChrystal, the result of similar indiscretions. The departure of General Mattis, a cerebral Marine despite a martial image, was announced by the Pentagon some nine months before his tenure was up, for reasons that may have to do planning for an attack on Iranian nuclear facilities.[21]

The mission of these proconsuls is not just the conduct of military operations and the development of contingency plans for war. Though they have large staffs for this, their intelligence components are even larger, and they see their role as more than military. At CENTCOM in late 1999, it was concern over the political aftermath of an invasion of Iraq, not the military task of taking down a regime which he knew lacked all conviction, that led General Tony Zinni to sponsor a week-long seminar in the Washington beltway for senior national security bureaucrats, almost all civilian, from State, Defense, CIA, and the White House staff. The exercise was designed to explore the difficulties involved in governing a post Saddam Hussein Iraq in the event of an invasion, but when the time came its conclusions were ignored by the Bush administration. (There is no cure for arrogance and stupidity.[22]) If similar efforts have not been underway at CENTCOM with regard to the aftermath of an American attack on Iran, its battle staff would be derelict in its duty.

Headquartered in Hawaii, the Pacific Command is a rival for CENTCOM in importance. Its commander, invariably an Admiral, plays a disproportionate diplomatic role, usually in alliance with the Asia hands of the State Department, but occasionally in competition with them. Overreaching by China in the South China sea and elsewhere provides PACOM and U.S. diplomacy with the ability to exercise a balancing role in Asia, and the restraint which has been exercised in the Pacific theater is in sharp contrast with the disasters in Iraq and Afghanistan.

DOI: 10.1057/9781137298553.0006

It is standard fare at these military establishments and in the Pentagon to deplore the fact that the weakness of the State Department has required them to step into political and diplomatic waters. Most of those who do so are in good faith, but the unified commands are genetically engineered to fill the void left by the State Department's retreat, and there should be no surprise in the fact that this is exactly what they have done. A marginalized State Department is simply not in a position to compete with these purposeful military behemoths, with their staffs of thousands of capable and hard-charging officers and large budgets.

Notes

1   http://articles.washingtonpost.com/2012-08-23/opinions/35492622_1_east-china-seas-military-budget-south-china. For a fuller exposition of the concept from which its classified dimensions can be inferred, see the article by the Air Force Chief of Staff and the Chief of Naval Operations Air-Sea Battle Promoting Stability in an Era of Uncertainty, General Norton A. Schwartz, USAF, and Admiral Jonathan W. Greenert, USN, at http://www.the-american-interest.com/article.cfm?piece=1212. The extent to which the Defense Department embraces A2AD as a capability to be funded is likely to be a major bone of contention in the upcoming Quadrennial Defense Review, pitting the services against each other in the scramble for resources. The Chinese are already up in arms about the concept, as the question posed by a Chinese journalist to General Dempsey in a recent public appearance shows: http://csis.org/event/thoughts-future-gulf.

2   For one version of this notion, cf. http://www.strategicstudiesinstitute.army.mil/era-of-persistent-conflict/.

3   According to its manufacturer, Lockheed Martin, the next generation fighter aircraft, the F-35, is being built in 47 states and Puerto Rico. It will come in three models, one each for the Air Force, for the Navy, and the Marine Corps. The three states left out must lack Congressional clout.

4   http://www.nytimes.com/2012/06/01/world/middleeast/obama-ordered-wave-of-cyberattacks-against-iran.html?pagewanted=all Sanger had access to senior White House officials. The Washington adage is that a ship leaks from the top.

5   http://thecable.foreignpolicy.com/posts/2013/09/24/obamas_favorite_general_stripped_of_his_security_clearance.

6   http://www.washingtonpost.com/world/national-security/us-spy-agencies-mounted-231-offensive-cyber-operations-in-2011-documents-show/2013/08/30/d090a6ae-119e-11e3-b4cb-fd7ce041d814_story.html.

DOI: 10.1057/9781137298553.0006

7   Alexander's March 12, 2013 testimony before the Senate Armed Services
    Committee will have been closely read in foreign capitals, from
    Beijing to Tehran to London: http://www.armed-services.senate.gov/
    statemnt/2013/03%20March/Alexander%2003-12-13.pdf.

8   On March 12, 2013, http://www.dni.gov/files/documents/Intelligence%20
    Reports/WWTA%20Remarks%20as%20delivered%2012%20Mar%202013.pdf.

9   http://www.armed-services.senate.gov/statemnt/2013/03%20March/
    Alexander%2003-12-13.pdf.

10 See the Congressional testimony of Christopher Painter, March 23, 2013: http://
    docs.house.gov/meetings/FA/FA14/20130321/100547/HHRG-113-FA14-Wstate-
    PainterC-20130321.pdf. The White House commissioned a top-to-bottom
    review of the Federal Government's efforts to defend our information
    and communications infrastructure, which resulted in a report titled *The
    Cyberspace Policy Review*. To implement the results of this review, the President
    has appointed Howard Schmidt to serve at the U.S. Cybersecurity Coordinator
    and created the Cybersecurity Office within the National Security Staff, which
    works closely with the Federal Chief Information Officer Steven VanRoekel,
    the Federal Chief Technology Officer Todd Park, and the National Economic
    Council.

11 http://www.whitehouse.gov/assets/documents/Cyberspace_Policy_Review_
    final.pdf.

12 http://www.nytimes.com/2013/03/22/us/influential-ex-aide-to-obama-voices-
    concern-on-drone-strikes.html?pagewanted=all.

13 For the details see Mark Mazzetti, *The Way of the Knife*, 2013, 291–293.

14 The military's earlier term for its peacetime operations was "shaping", a
    battlefield metaphor which has been mostly abandoned.

15 See the posture statement to the Senate Armed Services Committee of the
    SOCOM Commander, Admiral William McRaven, March 6, 2012, http://
    www.fas.org/irp/congress/2012_hr/030612mcraven.pdf.

16 The reader may easily imagine how this is done. For a useful inventory of the
    Pentagon's public affairs activities and some sense of the cost, including of
    SOCOM's MIST teams, see the study by the Stimson Center, at http://www.
    stimson.org/images/uploads/research-pdfs/Pentagon_as_pitchman.pdf.

17 http://www.washingtonpost.com/opinions/david-ignatius-drawing-
    down-but-still-projecting-power/2013/03/29/591ebe30-9895-11e2-814b-
    063623d80a60_story.html?wpisrc=nl_headlines.

18 These drone activities were so extensive that tiny Djibouti recently ordered a
    closure of its air space to them (http://articles.washingtonpost.com/2013-09-24/
    world/42357265_1_drone-operations-drone-flights-drone-strikes).

19 See Craig Whitlock, *The Washington Post*, July 8, 2012: http://www.
    washingtonpost.com/world/national-security/mysterious-fatal-

crash-provides-rare-glimpse-of-us-commandos-in-mali/2012/07/08/ gJQAGO71WW_story.html.

20 http://www.nytimes.com/2013/01/29/us/us-plans-base-for-surveillance-drones-in-northwest-africa.html.

21 See http://ricks.foreignpolicy.com/posts/2013/01/25/mattis_vs_donilon_ wow_no_one_even_called_to_tell_him_he_was_being_replaced.

22 For chapter and verse see Tom Ricks, *Fiasco: The American Military Adventure in Iraq, 2003 to 2005,* 2006.

DOI: 10.1057/9781137298553.0006

5
Two Cheers for Striped Pants: Diplomacy for the 21st Century

Abstract: *Without American military power, the world would be much more Hobbesian and violent, but it is still a world of sovereign states. The authority which American ambassadors have over all military and intelligence operations provides a critical degree of coherence when it is well exercised. The sale of embassies to political contributors is deplorable, but so is the erosion of the competence and sense of mission of the Foreign Service which still provides some two-thirds of ambassadors. In the 21st century it will be necessary to move out of fortress embassies and incur a degree of risk, with governments held accountable for their protection. Without a reform of our diplomatic institutions, we may be drawn into more wars we don't need to fight.*

Pope, Laurence. *The Demilitarization of American Diplomacy: Two Cheers for Striped Pants.* Basingstoke: Palgrave Macmillan, 2014.
DOI: 10.1057/9781137298553.0007.

For all of the beltway's alarums, the global environment is relatively benign for the United States. We have no competition as the world's leading state. Before China can emerge as a serious rival, it will have to address its sclerotic and corrupt political system and meet the growing demands of a restless population for a better life. There is conflict in today's world, and some of it is certainly persistent enough – the endless war in the Congo to which we pay little attention is a case in point, in addition to the ongoing slaughter of innocents in Syria – but there is less carnage than in the first half of the 20th century, with its destructive ideologies and terrible simplifications, before the long peace of the Cold War froze the international system in place. We have reorganized ourselves more or less successfully to deal with the threat of terrorism, and it is not an existential one in any case. The specious urgency of the bustling national security bureaucracy is often a product of its inflated self-importance.

The tone is set at the Defense Department, which promotes a vision of the world as an inherently dangerous place. The Obama administration has not issued a so-called National Security Strategy since 2010, although by law it is required to do so on an annual basis, an indication of how little such documents matter, but a new one is said to be imminent. When it comes out, like its predecessors it will be a general document with millenarian goals, since a real strategy would require reconciling ends with means and accepting limits, and Presidents prefer to avoid hard choices until it is absolutely necessary to make them. (They also have a sensible aversion to announcing plans which are bound to change in response to circumstances.) The 2010 version contained the notion of a strategic shift from the Middle East to Asia. This has been largely rhetorical in practice, as events in Syria and Egypt, and the threat of nuclear proliferation in Iran, have contrived to pin the administration down in the Middle East. Real strategy documents are written at the Defense Department.

Typical of the genre is the so-called Capstone Concept for Joint Operations announced in September of 2012 by the Chairman of the Joint Chiefs, General Martin Dempsey, as his vision for how the U.S. military should operate through 2020.[1] It paints a picture of a dark world, "a future security environment likely to be more unpredictable, complex, and potentially dangerous than today", requiring "globally integrated operations" – a permanent presence on the cyber barricades, as we defend against attacks by "networked" adversaries. This dark vision of formless fears and shadowy adversaries coexists uneasily with national

DOI: 10.1057/9781137298553.0007

security strategy developed at the White House full of the sunlit uplands of democracy, but it is the military-intelligence complex that holds sway in today's Washington. Utopian pronouncements from the White House are mainly for public consumption.

Whether the Defense Department's dark vision will hold sway in an era of budget cuts and limited resources is open to question. The President's decision not to use military force to punish the Syrian regime for using chemical weapons against its own population has exposed a vein of war-weariness in the country bordering on neo-isolationism. An American withdrawal from military commitments around the world would not be without consequences. As a thought experiment, imagine for a moment that U.S. military power had not been present over the last fifty years in Asia, Europe, and the Middle East. Who would have played a balancing role in the Pacific, holding the ring against a newly assertive China, protecting democracy in Japan, and allowing it to develop in South Korea? Would a prosperous and peaceful Europe have developed, and the Soviet empire have collapsed, without the NATO alliance and the presence of U.S. forces on the continent as a token of American resolve and leadership? Despite misconceived military adventures in Iraq and Afghanistan over the past decade, even in the Middle East American military power has been a force for global stability. In the absence of American naval power in the Persian Gulf, conflict between Arabs and Persians would probably have destabilized the global economy long ago, and Israel might well have been overwhelmed. Without the hard power of the United States, the world would be a good deal more Hobbesian and violent. The threat inflation routinely indulged in the Pentagon at the prospect of defense cuts should not obscure the fact that American military power remains central to the preservation of the mostly peaceful world we have today. Today's special forces are a sharp sword forged in a decade of war. No President should be asked to forego their use. The danger is that they will be put to uses for which they were not intended.

The same is true for the so-called intelligence community. While one can question a price tag of $75 billion, and the vast intelligence bureaucracy which has arisen since 9/11, including the duplicative superstructure known as the National Intelligence Council and the fact that we apparently now have more spies than diplomats, it is hard to argue with the premise that the country needs both a good espionage service and the ability to make sense of the world.

DOI: 10.1057/9781137298553.0007

In time, we may find that there are worse things than a world of nation-states, with all its frustrations. There is perhaps something in Jean-Marie Guéhenno's prediction that the demise of sovereign states would also mark the end of democracy. When the usually sensible Chairman of the Joint Staff, General Martin Dempsey, picks up the fashionable notion that "power is shifting below and beyond the state",[2] when there is serious talk in military circles of an Air Sea Battle doctrine involving cyberwar and drones, and when a preemptive attack on Iranian nuclear facilities is in the air, these are dangerous illusions. Network utopianism and a global military presence are both facets of American exceptionalism.

The weakness of the State Department and the decline of the Foreign Service have left a void in the national security structure which no other institutions are in a position to fill, though the military-intelligence complex is trying to do just that. The problem is not money. In a federal budget largely consumed by entitlement programs, diplomacy is a minor line item amounting to only a little more that 1% of the total, including foreign assistance to states like Israel, Egypt, and Pakistan. The personnel costs of the State Department and USAID are some $4 billion a year – less than half of the annual SOCOM budget, let alone the half-a-trillion dollars we spend annually on the Defense Department. The issue is one of mission and leadership.

Reforming the State Department and the Foreign Service is feasible given even a modest amount of political will, and it can be done without reinventing the entire national security bureaucracy. As a talent pool the Foreign Service is still a cut above most federal bureaucracies, a cross section of young and intelligent men and women with a commitment to public service.[3] Attempts to dilute the quality of this group by allowing entry at the middle grades, bypassing the competitive examination, have not succeeded so far, though the Foreign Service Act of 1980 is under threat both on the Hill and inside the State Department from those who do not believe that we need a diplomatic service. The Foreign Service enjoys a reasonably good public reputation in most quarters, and many capable and dedicated people are still drawn to diplomacy as a career. The Wikileaks cables had the unintended consequence of drawing public attention to the relatively high quality of at least some diplomatic reporting. The deaths in 2012 in Libya of Ambassador Chris Stevens, and of the twenty-five-year-old Anne Smedingoff in Afghanistan in 2013, have reminded the country of the sacrifices made by FSOs and their families. There is a reservoir of public good will to build on. Most outsiders, even

DOI: 10.1057/9781137298553.0007

those who are well-informed, assume that the Foreign Service is still the dominant institution in the State Department. They are surprised and disturbed to hear that this is no longer the case. The decline of both institutions is an open secret in Washington; sooner or later the rest of the country will learn of it as well.

Given a modicum of leadership from the Secretary of State and the support of the President, there could be the beginning of change, but it will be a long road. The Foreign Service is uniquely positioned to counter Washington's propensity for making foreign policy without reference to foreigners. Traditional diplomacy's monopoly on specialized information about the outside world has been lost, but this was never the source of its comparative advantage. In a world where information moves with the speed of thought, the issue is usually not what is happening, but what should be done about it. The role of a diplomatic service is to help chart a course for the ship of state through rough seas, and sometimes even to advise that a different course might be preferable given the circumstances – for there are always circumstances. A functioning foreign ministry and a sound diplomatic service are essential components of a healthy national security system, and their weakness contributes to the militarization of our approach to the world. When all you have is a hammer, everything looks like a nail.

A reinvented and renewed American diplomatic service will not spring into existence fully armed, Minerva from the brow of Zeus. Like any professional body, it is the product of experience, training, and a sense of mission and competence. The dumbing down of our diplomatic institutions is part of a larger trend involving the delegitimization of public service in the era of distrust for government and all its works. The Tea Party forgets that our founding fathers were sophisticated men of the enlightenment who took diplomacy seriously. Jefferson's copy of Callières's diplomatic manual is in the Library of Congress. At a time of divided government, it is all the more important for institutions like the Foreign Service to be able to provide a measure of continuity across changes in administration. The outside world cannot always be relied on to wait on our pleasure while we argue interminably amongst ourselves. Max Weber's bureaucracies have their uses.

Reforming the State Department and the Foreign Service will require giving our diplomats additional breathing room and the ability to operate. Today they are too often surrounded by concertina wire and contract

DOI: 10.1057/9781137298553.0007

armies with guns, inside the fortress embassies we have built around the world. Since the suicide bombing of our Embassy in Nairobi in 1998, a high rise building on a busy street, the State Department has been engaged in an expensive worldwide effort to harden Embassy defenses against attack. Among other things, this involves a 100-foot setback from public streets, high walls, and the control of visitors at a distant perimeter where they are searched and relieved of their cell phones. The unintended consequence has been to close off our embassies from the world around them. When both American citizens and foreign contacts find it unpleasant to approach their forbidding gates, more meetings on the outside are required if any business is to be done, and this only adds to the risk involved. Closeted personnel lacking a feel for the world outside the walls will be unsafe in the outside world no matter how high and how well guarded those walls are. In war zones like Iraq and Afghanistan, though many chafe at the restrictions, Foreign Service Officers have become too accustomed to life in hermetically sealed compounds from which they are allowed to sortie forth only under heavily armed guard. Part of the answer must be to hold governments responsible for the protection of our people, instead of trying to turn embassies into extraterritorial bases. If foreign governments are not willing to protect the embassies we send them or are unable to do so, perhaps they should not be there. They are likely to be incapable of diplomatic work in that situation in any case, and the platforms they provide for the operations of other agencies may have to be dispensed with in order not to put our people at unacceptable risk.

In the self-indulgent orgy of partisan blame-mongering after the Benghazi attacks of September 2012, we have forgotten that threats to our personnel abroad are not new. In 1967, the consulate in Benghazi was overrun and its personnel barely escaped with their lives. In 1973, our ambassador to Khartoum, Cleo Noel and his deputy Curt Moore were murdered by Palestinian terrorists. Ambassador Roger Davies was killed by a sniper's bullet in Cyprus in 1974. Ambassador Frank Meloy was murdered in Beirut in 1976, with Foreign Service Officer Robert Waring. In 1979, our ambassador to Afghanistan, Spike Dubs, was killed when Afghan forces and their Soviet advisors engaged in a gunfight with his kidnappers. Our entire Embassy in Tehran was taken hostage and held for 444 days, and its personnel were badly mistreated, some to the point of torture. In 1983, the Embassy in Beirut was bombed, killing 63 people, including 17 Americans, and it was attacked again the following

DOI: 10.1057/9781137298553.0007

year despite hardened defenses. After the murders in Benghazi, we need to relearn the lesson that diplomacy is a dangerous business, even as we take precautions to minimize the risks which are inevitable.

Does the quality of our diplomats really matter that much? That is a matter of opinion perhaps, and some readers may not be persuaded by the arguments here which are necessarily general in nature. The Foreign Affairs Oral History Collection is an indispensable resource for anyone who is curious about what diplomats do, at http://memory.loc.gov/ammem/collections/diplomacy/. It includes an interview with the late Richard B. Parker. As a young Army officer in World War II, Parker was taken prisoner during the Battle of the Bulge and somehow escaped, making his way back after two months behind enemy lines. When I met him in 1973 he was the Deputy Chief of Mission in Rabat, and I was a junior political officer. Having been trained in the local dialect of Arabic, I rejected the apartments the embassy offered in the European part of the city, and took a traditional house in the center of the walled Arab quarter, inaccessible by car. (The rent was $60 a month, and the embassy was probably overpaying.) This would be inconceivable today, and even then the outraged security officer at the embassy demanded that I be ordered to move out. Summoning me to his office, Parker asked why I hadn't invited him to visit. I stammered some excuse, convinced that I had violated an unwritten rule of protocol. He and his wife came by for lunch, and I never heard another word from the security officer. Parker went on to serve as ambassador in Algeria, Lebanon, and Morocco. In Algeria he made a close connection with the dour revolutionary who was the head of state, Houari Boumediene, arguing with him in fluent Arabic, sometimes to good effect. In Lebanon he fought hard for the extension of Lebanese government control throughout the country. The King of Morocco found him troublesome, but in his hands the honor of the United States was always safe. With notable exceptions, there are not many Foreign Service Officers like Dick Parker today, and he would not thrive in the contemporary State Department.

One element to build on in is the unity of command deriving from the authority of ambassadors over all U.S. government operations. A forceful and experienced chief of mission in the field, or a career official in Washington with the ear of the Secretary of State for that matter, can have disproportionate influence. Most ambassadors still come from the career Foreign Service, though there is no guarantee that this will always be the case, and a recent tendency to bypass career State Department

DOI: 10.1057/9781137298553.0007

officers in favor of the ranks of USAID and other government agencies suggests an institutional lack of faith in the career service.[4] The resort to retired officers to fill in as chiefs of mission is another sign of trouble.

The scramble for embassies at the beginning of the second Obama term has resulted in the nomination of a large number of political ambassadors in payment of campaign debts, in countries from Belgium to Spain, Australia to Japan. A former career Foreign Service Officer and ambassador, Dennis Jett, has compiled a useful study of the sale of embassies – more precisely their award to serious bundlers of campaign funds.[5] That this is a deplorable practice is generally admitted; that it will not end any time soon is also generally acknowledged. Ignoring the (toothless, admittedly) provision of the 1980 Foreign Service Act which declares that political contributions must not be a factor in the naming of ambassadors, in its second term the Obama Administration has rewarded campaign donors with embassies so shamelessly, without the slightest attention to their qualifications, that it would make Boss Tweed of Tammany Hall blush. At the close of 2013, over half of its second term ambassadorial appointments have been political.[6] As campaign debts are paid, this imbalance is likely to be restored to something closer to historical levels, but it is hard to escape the impression that it reflects disdain at the White House for both the position and the Foreign Service, and not just politics as usual. Is it perhaps also the case that capable and assertive chiefs of mission are seen as a threat to the primacy of the national security staff at the White House?

How much damage an incompetent chief of mission can do is open to debate. Our closest friends are accustomed to our ways. They can always use their own embassy in Washington, usually headed by one of their best career officers, for serious business. The Italian-American connection operates on many levels, and it has survived a long series of political ambassadors in Rome. It is also true that some political appointees will succeed as chiefs of mission when they are supported by a strong career staff. Jon Huntsman was a better ambassador to Singapore and China than he was a Presidential candidate. Caroline Kennedy can hardly do worse in Tokyo than her grandfather did at the Court of Saint James, where he was a voice for the appeasement of Hitler, or more recently her aunt Jean Kennedy Smith in Dublin, where according to her nemesis in London, unusually at the time a career officer, she was a strident voice in favor of the IRA.[7] (The greater danger may be that she will become the creature of the Japanese foreign

DOI: 10.1057/9781137298553.0007

ministry.) Like the poor, political appointees will always be with us. Some will be competent, some less so – and the same thing goes for career officers.[8]

Hillary Clinton's QDDR calls for ambassadors to be chief executive officers, but that would be a demotion. Embassies are autocracies with a purpose, collections of people with widely varying responsibilities few of whom work for the State Department these days. Ambassadors have no board of directors and no shareholders to hold them to account when the stock price falls. In a fragmented and contentious national security bureaucracy, the President's injunction to all ambassadors to exercise "full responsibility for the direction, coordination, and supervision of all Government executive branch employees in that country" is a powerful tool in experienced hands.[9] These ambassadorial authorities are real, not ceremonial, and ambassadors represent the President, not the State Department. A wise chief of mission will wear this authority lightly, and seek to persuade rather than to compel, in the knowledge that if she tolerates defiance of her authority she stands to lose it. Like the captain of a naval vessel, she should expect to be held fully to account if the ship of state goes aground – whether or not she was on the bridge.

Outsiders sometimes wonder whether diplomacy is obsolete in the age of instant communication. A moment's reflection is enough to show why this is not the case. The world is a busy and complicated place, and senior Washington officials from the President on down are capable of attending to only a few problems at a time, often driven by the false urgencies of the 24/7 news cycle. Like seven-year-olds playing soccer they flock to the ball of the moment, leaving the rest of the vast field unattended. When a crisis somewhere concentrates the minds of the President's senior advisors, they tend to focus on the tactical details, which are often easier to think about than the larger policy questions involved. Unity of command in a given country is the sole province of the chief of mission. There is no one else who can see the whole field of play. It is rare for the State Department to instruct a good ambassador in any but the most general way about the conduct of bilateral relations, and communications run in two directions in the age of secure video conferences. A capable chief of mission in full possession of her portfolio will often be able to manage the beltway, and most operations in the field cannot be directed from Washington, involving as they often do rival agencies of government, without constant supervision from busy deputies of cabinet departments or even their principals, which

DOI: 10.1057/9781137298553.0007

is usually impractical. Ambassadors are very hard to remove, and they are rarely relieved because of disagreements over policy. Character flaws magnified by the seductive allure of the position are more likely to be the cause. The temptation to confuse the office with the person is not easily resisted, and this applies to amateurs and professionals alike.

So what is to be done, an impatient reader may ask? I have no ten-point plan to offer. The American Academy of Diplomacy, a group of retired ambassadors, has made useful recommendations about more training and mentoring for our diplomats, and it is at work on a project to address what many see as a crisis of competence in the contemporary Foreign Service. The American Foreign Service Association is launching a similar effort, but these commendable initiatives often amount to preaching to the choir. Many people in contemporary Washington, in the think tanks, in government, and on the Hill, are unpersuaded that we need a diplomatic service at all. Secretary Clinton created a Foreign Affairs Advisory Board of eminent persons on the model of the influential Defense Policy Board. It has done little or nothing to date. It could be tasked by her successor to consider whether in the 21st century we need a first-rate diplomatic service, though the White House might see even so modest an effort as insubordination, and there would be resistance from inside the State Department itself from those who see the Foreign Service as an anachronism.

Recognition of the fact that the United States has a dysfunctional foreign ministry would be the beginning of wisdom. That the unlovely edifice at 23rd and C Street in Foggy Bottom is mostly relegated to internal housekeeping and its globalizing fantasies, tweeting past the grave while policy and operations are centered in the White House, is not in the interest of the President. His duties as commander-in-chief should not require him to make daily course corrections, or to write out a lawyerly "terms sheet" in a negotiation over troop levels with his own generals, as was the case in the endless and largely inconclusive review of Afghanistan policy in Obama's first term. A delegation of authority to the Secretary of State would allow him to stand above the beltway alarums, as he shows every indication of wanting to do, and not be constantly dragged back into the relentless frenzy of the news cycle. Dwight Eisenhower was perhaps the last American President who understood the making of strategy. He cultivated the image of being above the battle, but there was never any doubt about who was in charge. It is in the President's interest to have a strong Secretary of State. To perform that role effectively, the

DOI: 10.1057/9781137298553.0007

Secretary needs more than a personal staff of Congressional staffers and Washington lawyers. He needs a functioning institution under his control, capable of standing up to the military-intelligence complex in the corridors of power, with a strong admixture of professionals at the top. This would be a useful topic of discussion between the President and his Secretary of State; only they can say whether it is a likely one. Secretary Kerry's tireless efforts in the Middle East and elsewhere illustrate the old adage that optimism is to the diplomat as courage is to the soldier. If he does decide to grasp this institutional nettle, he will need all the optimism he can muster.

A reform effort will have to be grounded in the emerging reality of the 21st century, not in nostalgia for the past. That indispensable old Prussian von Clausewitz, whose *On War* ought to be in the traveling library of diplomats, wrote that the first question to be asked by generals and statesmen is not what kind of war it should be, but what kind of war it is.[10] The landscape of the 21st century is coming into clearer focus after two failed wars. The information age and cyberspace are new realities, but fundamentally it remains a world of states, not networks. American leadership will be as indispensable in it as ever, and exercising that leadership will require acting in coalitions the United States may sometimes be able to convene but rarely control. The shrill voices on both the right and the left who advocated a global American imperium as we massed divisions on the Iraqi border are chastened now, and a retreat from the burdens of leadership may be the greater danger. As we continue to wrestle with our role in the world, something like a strategy will emerge – not from what we say, but from what we do.

One thing is clear. It will be what the evidence of our senses tells us: a world of sovereign nations. The world is not flat. Other states will develop antidotes to the drone technology which compromises their sovereignty. Threats which arise in cyberspace will not be susceptible to a purely military response. In the Middle East, the vestiges of the post Ottoman state system are disappearing in an orgy of ethnic cleansing, a process which may take a generation. Having sown the wind with our neglect of the Palestinian-Israeli conflict, we may live to reap the whirlwind. The Arab awakening has life in it yet, with potential consequences for Saudi Arabia and the Persian Gulf. An American attack on Iran could feed the flames. In Asia, there is the possibility of a U.S.–China confrontation at some point, as two great powers test their strength against each other. In a complex global system, rising powers like India and Brazil will demand

DOI: 10.1057/9781137298553.0007

their share of influence. The UN Security Council which reflects the world of 1945 will need to be reformed or it will cease to have any moral or legal authority.

Dealing with these challenges will require both tactical agility and strategic restraint. Restoring the atrophied diplomatic reflexes of a muscle-bound national security state would help, but in the end it will come down to the kind of people we are. Do we believe that we stand outside history? That we are not bound by the rules that bind others? That the sovereignty of other states is negotiable, while ours is sacrosanct? That military dominance is the principal virtue of our good land? Are we the country of Guantanamo and Abu Ghraib, of torture and the excesses of extrajudicial renditions which have stained our honor?

President Obama has tried to set a new course. His speech at the National Defense University on May 23, 2013,[11] contained some of the arguments of this book, but it did not address the institutional imbalances which have placed our national security structure on a permanent war footing. His rhetorical shift away from the global war on terror belies the fact that with his Presidency in its sixth year it continues in all but name. Neither Obama nor his new Secretary of State has shown any understanding of the institutional reforms which will be necessary to demilitarize the conduct of American diplomacy around the world.

At our best, an idealism tempered with a pragmatic sense of the limits of power has governed American conduct in the world. Today, our exposed city on a hill looks out on a rapidly changing landscape with as much promise as threat. The weakness of our civilian foreign policy institutions has invited the intrusion of the military-intelligence complex into the spheres of politics and diplomacy, and in the process our republican traditions have been militarized to a degree our ancestors would find shocking. At the end of an unhappy decade of war, perhaps the time has come to restore the institutions of American diplomacy for a world of sovereign states.

Notes

1   http://www.jcs.mil//content/files/2012-09/092812122654_CCJO_JF2020_FINAL.pdf.
2   http://breakingdefense.com/2013/03/18/cjcs-gen-dempsey-signals-strategy-change-touts-decline-of-state.

DOI: 10.1057/9781137298553.0007

3   The written entry examination was revised in 2007 by the management
    consultant McKinsey to downplay knowledge of the outside world in favor
    of "managerial" prowess, but an oral examination remains. See http://www.
    foreignpolicy.com/articles/2008/10/09/the_diplomatic_surge?page=0,2.

4   Ambassadors from the Foreign Commercial Service and the Foreign
    Agricultural Service, as well as from USAID have been named. They are
    included in the total of career officers.

5   "What Price the Court of St. James? Political Influences on Ambassadorial
    Postings of the United States of America" with J. W. Fedderke, at http://www.
    econrsa.org/system/files/publications/working_papers/working_paper_234.
    pdf. It contains a useful appendix showing that from the Eisenhower
    years through the administration of George W. Bush, the ratio of career
    appointments to political was about two to one. In the first Obama
    administration, roughly 70% of ambassadors were career: http://www.
    afsa.org/ambassadorlist.aspx. A recent statement by the American Foreign
    Service association notes, however, that over the past three decades "85% of
    ambassadorial appointments to major European countries and Japan, and
    nearly 60% of appointments to a wider group of emerging global powers
    such as Brazil, Russia, India, and China, have been political." http://www.
    afsa.org/ambassadors.aspx.

6   The running total is at http://www.afsa.org/secondterm.aspx. So far 54% of
    second term nominees have been campaign donors. As a historical matter,
    both the Clinton and Bush Administrations appointed about 70% of
    ambassadors from the career service, compared to 63.5% so far during the
    first and second Obama terms.

7   See Ambassador Seitz's memoir *Over Here,* Orion Publishing, 1998.

8   Callières told a story about the Duke of Tuscany, who is said to have
    complained to a visiting Venetian that the Venetian Ambassador to his court
    was a fool. Unfortunately we have lots of fools in Venice, said the Venetian.
    We have our share in Tuscany too, said the Duke, but we don't send them
    abroad to represent us.

9   Quoted in a 2009 paper for the National Defense University by former
    Ambassador Edward Marks and Christopher J. Lamb, one of many such
    efforts at interagency reform at the time, is at http://www.ndu.edu/inss/
    docuploaded/INSS%20Strategic%20Perspectives%202_Lamb%20.pdf. It is
    illustrated by a photo of President Obama and his team being briefed by
    secure video conference by then Ambassador to Afghanistan, LTG (retired)
    Karl Eikenberry.

10 "Now, the first, the grandest, and most decisive act of judgment which the
    Statesman and General exercises is rightly to understand in this respect the
    War in which he engages, not to take it for something, or to wish to make of

it something, which by the nature of its relations it is impossible for it to be." Karl von Clausewitz, *On War*.

11   "I believe, however, that the use of force must be seen as part of a larger discussion we need to have about a comprehensive counterterrorism strategy – because for all the focus on the use of force, force alone cannot make us safe. We cannot use force everywhere that a radical ideology takes root; and in the absence of a strategy that reduces the wellspring of extremism, a perpetual war – through drones or Special Forces or troop deployments – will prove self-defeating, and alter our country in troubling ways." http://www.whitehouse.gov/the-press-office/2013/05/23/remarks-president-national-defense-university.

DOI: 10.1057/9781137298553.0007

Selected Bibliography

Acheson, D. *Present at the Creation*. W. W. Norton & Company, 1987.

Albright, M. *Madam Secretary*. HarperCollins, 2003.

Alter, J. *The Center Holds*. Simon and Schuster, 2013.

Bacevich, A. J. *Washington Rules*. Metropolitan Books, 2010.

Baker, J. A., and T. M. Defrank. *The Politics of Diplomacy: Revolution, War, and Peace, 1989–1992*. Putnam Pub Group, 1995.

Berridge, G. R. *British Diplomacy in Turkey*. Martinus Nijhoff Publishers, 2009.

Berridge, G. R. *Diplomacy*. Palgrave Macmillan, 2010.

Berridge, G. R. *Embassies in Armed Conflict*. Continuum, 2012.

Berridge, G. R. and L. Lloyd. *The Palgrave Macmillan Dictionary of Diplomacy*. Palgrave Macmillan, 2012.

Buren, P. V. *We Meant Well: How I Helped Lose the Battle for the Hearts and Minds of the Iraqi People*. Metropolitan Books, 2011.

Callières, F. D. *On Negotiating with Sovereigns: The Art of Diplomacy*. Holmes & Meier Pub, 1983.

Chandrasekaran, R. *Imperial Life in the Emerald City*. Random House LLC, 2007.

Chandrasekaran, R. *Little America*. Random House LLC, 2013.

Clausewitz, C. V. *On War*. Princeton University Press, 1989.

Glain, S. *State Vs. Defense*. Random House LLC, 2011.

Guéhenno, J. *La fin de la démocratie*, 1993.

DOI: 10.1057/9781137298553.0008

Hammes, T. X. *The Sling and the Stone*. Zenith Imprint, 2006.

Isaacson, W. *Kissinger*. Simon and Schuster, 1992.

Kennedy, C. S., and D. Mak. *American Ambassadors in a Troubled World*. Greenwood Publishing Group, 1992.

Kissinger, H. *White House Years*. Little Brown, 1979.

Kissinger, H. *Diplomacy*. Simon and Schuster, 1994.

Kissinger, H. *Years of Upheaval*. Simon & Schuster, 1999.

Mann, J. *The Obamians*. Viking Press, 2012.

Mazzetti, M. *The Way of the Knife*. Penguin Press HC, 2013.

Murphy, R. D. *Diplomat among Warriors*. Greenwood Pub Group, 1964.

Neumann (Ret), R. E. *The Other War*. Inc., 2009.

Parker, R. B. *Uncle Sam in Barbary*. University Press Of Florida, 2004.

Pillar, P. R. *Terrorism and U.S. Foreign Policy*. The Brookings Institution, 2001.

Pope, L. *François de Callières*, Republic of Letters Publishing, 2010.

Rice, Condoleezza. *No Higher Honor: A Memoir of My Years in Washington*. Broadway Paperbacks, 2011.

Ricks, T. E. *Fiasco*. Penguin, 2006.

Sanger, D. E. *Confront and Conceal*. Random House LLC, 2012.

Schake, K. N. *State of Disrepair*. Hoover Institution Press, 2012.

Schlesinger, A. M. *A Thousand Days: John F. Kennedy in the White House*. Houghton Mifflin Harcourt, 1965.

Schmitt, E., and T. Shanker. *Counterstrike*. St. Martin's Griffin, 2011.

Shultz, G. *Turmoil and Triumph*. Simon and Schuster, 1993.

Sullivan, J. G. *Embassies under Siege*. Potomac Books Inc, 1995.

Stearns, M. *Talking to Strangers*. Princeton University Press, 1995.

Seitz, R. *Over Here*. Orion Publishing, 1998.

Wissing, D. A. *Funding the Enemy*. Prometheus Books, 2012.

Woodward, B. *Obama's Wars*. Simon & Schuster, 2010.

Zinni, T. *The Battle for Peace*. Palgrave Macmillan, 2006.

DOI: 10.1057/9781137298553.0008

Index

DOI: 10.1057/9781137298553.0009

DOI: 10.1057/9781137298553.0009

DOI: 10.1057/9781137298553.0009

CPSIA information can be obtained at www.ICGtesting.com
Printed in the USA
BVOW08*0114190214

345317BV00002B/12/P